The Quality of Cranes

A LITTLE BOOK OF CRANE LORE

FACTS, FOLKLORE
& FANCIFUL TALES

by Betsy Didrickson

Published by and available from:
The International Crane Foundation
E11376 Shady Lane Road
Baraboo, Wisconsin 53913 USA
www.savingcranes.org

All proceeds from the sale of this book benefit global crane
conservation efforts by the International Crane Foundation.

Sustainable Design and Print
This book was designed by Loose Animals Art & Design. Loose Animals works with eco-friendly companies
to create publications that use resources efficiently before, during, and after production. The paper is
made and the book is printed a short distance from the delivery point – reducing its carbon footprint.
This book is printed with vegetable inks on acid-free Cougar Opaque paper that is Forest Stewardship
Council certified. The manufacturer, Domtar Paper, makes an annual contribution from the sale of
Cougar products to the World Wildlife Fund to support conservation efforts. The liner sheet is recycled,
acid and lignin-free Green Seal certified Royal Fiber Sunflower paper. The font is Goudy Old Style.

"Our ability to perceive quality in nature begins, as in art, with the pretty. It expands through successive stages of the beautiful to values as yet uncaptured by language. The quality of cranes lies, I think, in this higher gamut, as yet beyond the reach of words."

— Aldo Leopold (1886-1948) *A Sand County Almanac*

DEDICATION

All who know the Crane, are aware of his resounding voice. The crane totem represents the echo-maker to the Crane Clan of the Ojibwe. The echo-maker personified is an eloquent leader and speaker for the clan. This book is dedicated to the International Crane Foundation's echo-maker, Dr. George Archibald

— B.D.

FOREWORD

Since 1997, I have had the privilege of being the Research Librarian at the Ron Sauey Memorial Library for Bird Conservation, the research library of the International Crane Foundation (ICF). Among other things, I answer a multitude of crane inquiries from around the world. Many of these requests are from biologists and researchers in faraway places and tend to be of a highly scientific nature. Scattered amongst the scientific requests, I noticed a growing number of inquiries about the symbolism and mythology of cranes.

I scrambled to find a comprehensive source of information to which I could refer people. Alas, there was no such thing. I began collecting and compiling tidbits from here and there – feathering my folklore nest over many years. I soon realized that cranes are much more to people than a species to check off their birding list; they truly are, as Aldo Leopold stated, in a *higher gamut... beyond the reach of words.*

Yet, here I am, attempting to collect words that express the qualities of cranes. I hope, in its humble way, this collection helps promote this most remarkable family of birds. "Lore" can be defined as knowledge gained through tradition or anecdote, as opposed to scientific means. For the most part, that is what is represented here, although each section was thoroughly researched and indexed. In addition to fables and tales, I've included many fun facts, answering some of the most frequently asked questions about cranes. I have summarized the actual folk tales in this book, but include references to more in-depth re-tellings and versions.

Each page is intended to be a self-contained "bit" of crane lore. Whether you are seeking a particular piece of information about cranes, or simply reading for pleasure – I hope you enjoy reading about... *the quality of cranes.*

— Betsy Didrickson

CHARISMATIC CRANES

Throughout the centuries, cranes have been revered by many of the cultures on each of the five continents where they live. It's no wonder then that today the crane is considered a flagship species by wildlife biologists. The term "flagship," as it relates to biological organisms, describes the promotion of charismatic species, such as cranes, as a way of mobilizing popular support for conservation. By helping a flagship species, other less flamboyant species are helped as well.

Biology aside, the desire to use the dramatic crane as a symbol in religion and art is understandable, as well as fascinating. The crane is a supermodel in the bird world — captivating humans with its long graceful neck and legs, rhythmic dancing, romantic synchronized unison calling, and perhaps most of all, its impressive stature. Cranes can be up to six feet tall (Sarus Crane) with a wingspan of over eight feet! The admiration that people throughout time have felt for cranes may, in the end, help save this endangered family of birds.

FIFTEEN SPECIES OF CRANES

SCIENTIFIC NAME	COMMON NAME	CONTINENT
Anthropoides paradisea[VU]	Blue or Stanley Crane	Africa
Anthropoides virgo[LC]	Demoiselle Crane	Africa, Asia
Balearica pavonina[NT]	Black Crowned Crane	Africa
Balearica regulorum[VU]	Grey Crowned Crane	Africa
Bugeranus carunculatus[VU]	Wattled Crane	Africa
Grus americana[EN]	Whooping Crane	North America
Grus antigone[VU]	Sarus Crane	Asia, Australia
Grus canadensis[LC]	Sandhill Crane	North America
Grus grus[LC]	Eurasian or Common Crane	Eurasia, Africa
Grus japonensis[EN]	Red-crowned or Japanese Crane	Asia
Grus leucogeranus[CR]	Siberian Crane	Asia
Grus monacha[VU]	Hooded Crane	Asia
Grus nigricollis[VU]	Black-necked Crane	Asia
Grus rubicunda[LC]	Brolga	Australia
Grus vipio[VU]	White-naped Crane	Asia

Conservation status based on: *The 2010 IUCN Red List of Threatened Species,* Version 2010.1 **www.redlist.org**

CRITICALLY ENDANGERED (CR) - A taxon is Critically Endangered when it is facing an extremely high risk of extinction in the wild in the immediate future.
ENDANGERED (EN) - A taxon is Endangered when it is not Critically Endangered but is facing a very high risk of extinction in the wild in the near future.
VULNERABLE (VU) - A taxon is Vulnerable when it is not Critically Endangered or Endangered but is facing a high risk of extinction in the wild in the medium-term future.
NEAR THREATENED (NT) – A taxon is Near Threatened when it has been evaluated against the criteria but does not qualify for Critically Endangered, Endangered, Vulnerable now, but is close to qualifying for, or is likely to qualify for a threatened category in the near future.
LEAST CONCERN (LC) – A taxon is Least Concern when it has been evaluated against the criteria and does not qualify for Critically Endangered, Endangered, Vulnerable or Near Threatened.

TREE OF CRANES

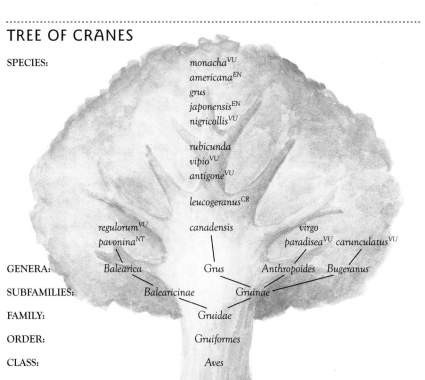

SPECIES:

monacha^{VU}
americana^{EN}
grus
japonensis^{EN}
nigricollis^{VU}

rubicunda
vipio^{VU}
antigone^{VU}

leucogeranus^{CR}

regulorum^{VU} canadensis   virgo
pavonina^{NT} paradisea^{VU} carunculatus^{VU}

GENERA: Balearica   Grus   Anthropoides   Bugeranus

SUBFAMILIES: Balearicinae   Gruinae

FAMILY: Gruidae

ORDER: Gruiformes

CLASS: Aves

Scientists have studied the DNA of the crane family and have found evidence to support the traditional view that crowned cranes (*Balearica*) are the most ancient lineage of extant gruids. The genera *Bugeranus* and *Anthropoides* are sister taxa. Three species of Australasian *Grus* (*antigone, rubicunda,* and *vipio*) form a cluster within that genera, as do five other *Grus* (*grus, monacha, nigricollis, japonensis,* and *americana*). The critically endangered Siberian Crane *Grus leucogeranus* is a sister group to those clusters, and the Sandhill Crane *Grus canadensis* is an isolated lineage without a close relative. (Krajewski, 1988)

ENDANGERED SPECIES ACT

In the 1960s many environmental laws were passed in the United States, but it wasn't until 1973, when Congress passed the Endangered Species Act (ESA), that important protection was granted to rare species. The ESA is considered by many to be the most important environmental law ever passed.

The ESA states that the Secretary of the Interior will determine if a species is **threatened, endangered,** or a **candidate** based on man-made factors affecting their continued existence. The status listings are similar to the IUCN Red List and apply to species outside of the U.S. as well.

Endangered: Species is in danger of extinction throughout all or a portion of its range.
Threatened: Species is likely to become endangered in the near future.
Candidate: Species may become endangered or threatened. The U.S. Fish & Wildlife Service keeps a list of candidate species.

Under the ESA, six crane species and two sub-species are listed as endangered:

- Whooping Crane
- Black-necked Crane
- Red-crowned Crane
- Siberian Crane
- Hooded Crane
- White-naped Crane
- Cuban Sandhill (sub species)
- Mississippi Sandhill Crane (sub species)

AN ANCIENT TRIBE

The beautiful crowned cranes are the most primitive of the living Gruidae (crane family). Primitive, no longer extant, species of crowned cranes, sub-family *Balearicinae,* date back in the fossil record to the Eocene period (55-33 million years ago). Archaeologists have discovered that at least 11 species of crowned cranes existed in Europe and North America over the last 50 million years. Because crowned cranes are not cold hardy, it is thought they died out in these areas as the earth cooled. Today they survive only in warm Africa.

Our appreciation of the crane grows
with the slow unraveling of earthly history.
His tribe, we now know, stems out of the remote Eocene.
The other members of the fauna in which he originated
are long since entombed within the hills.

— Aldo Leopold

OLDEST EXTANT BIRD?

The sub-family *Gruinae*, or typical cranes, first appears in the earth's fossil record in the Miocene period (from 24-5 million years ago). A Pliocene (5.4-2.4 million years ago) crane fossil found in Nebraska is thought by some to be structurally identical to the modern Sandhill Crane. If correct, this would make the Sandhill the oldest known bird species still surviving. The "Snake Creek" fossil was examined in 1928 by famed avian paleontologist Alexander Wetmore. Wetmore (1910-1978) was an ornithologist, author, and Secretary of the Smithsonian. He wrote, "The fossil has great importance in indicating an extraordinary stability in osteological form since it demonstrates the presence in the Pliocene of a crane identical in humeral characters with the existing Sandhill Crane, giving this type of bird the longest line of unchanged descent at present known on the North American continent in the class Aves." Today, some scientists believe that a fragment of a leg bone may not be sufficient to authenticate this statement, and yet the legend continues that the Sandhill is the oldest extant bird species.

As the oldest living bird species, the species that can claim the longest successful tenure on earth, the sandhill holds a pre-eminent position in the world of birds.

— Steven Grooms in *Cry of the Sandhill Crane*

CAVE CRANES

A nesting crane is depicted at the Tajo Segura Cave in southern Spain. Commenting on the 6,000-year-old artwork, Ron Sauey, Co-founder of the International Crane Foundation, wrote:

> *"It is significant because it represents the dawning*
> *of the long and wonderful history of the crane*
> *as an art form."*

A more recent discovery in Britain is the cave art at Creswell Crags, Derbyshire. The 12,000-year-old carvings depict two birds, possibly a crane or swan.

People in western Sweden painted pictographs of dancers performing a crane dance over 5,000 years ago.

NEOLITHIC CRANE COSTUME

In 1995, archaeologists discovered what appears to be an 8,500-year-old "crane costume" in a Neolithic Anatolian village in what is now Turkey. The costume was made from the feathered wing of a Eurasian Crane *Grus grus*.

The wing has holes drilled through it, presumably so it could be laced onto a human dancer's arms. Zooarchaeologists (anthropologists who study the role of animals in the lives of ancient peoples) speculate that the costume was likely used in a crane dance, possibly at a marriage ceremony. Cranes are renowned throughout the world for their lively dancing. Some of the societies known to imitate the crane dance around the world are the Ainu of Japan, the Khanti (also known as Hunty or Ostiaks) of Siberia, Aboriginal people of Australia, and the Ho-Chunk of North America.

CRANE MUSIC

The beautiful crane has long been depicted in the stories and artistry of humankind. In the late 1990s, archaeologists uncovered ancient flutes at Jiahu, Henan Province, China carved from the bone of a Red-crowned Crane. Jiahu was occupied from approximately 7,000 BC to 5,700 BC. Six intact multi-note flutes were recovered at the site. The best preserved of the 9,000-year-old flutes was played and an analysis performed. One might speculate that cranes had a profound meaning for the maker of the musical instrument. Indeed, a Ming dynasty treatise maintains, "From the thighbone of a crane excellent flutes can be made: their sound is clear, and in harmony with the sonorous tubes."

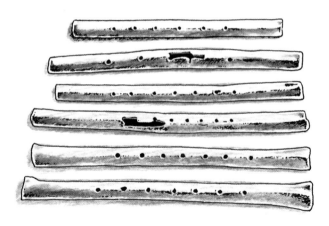

CALLING ALL CRANES!

The call of most cranes is a loud bugle, which is well suited for communication across vast wetlands or in large flocks of noisy migrating birds. The long trachea (windpipe) of many crane species loops and coils in the sternum, providing cranes with their impressive voice. This very long trachea is an adaptation for the production of not only loud, but very penetrating calls. Indeed, the Whooping Crane, or Hooping Crane as Audubon called it, possesses a windpipe over five feet long!

When we hear his call we hear no mere bird.

We hear the trumpet in the orchestra of evolution.

He is the symbol of our untamable past, of that incredible sweep of

millennia which underlies and conditions the daily affairs

of birds and men.

— Aldo Leopold

SYMBOLIC CRANES

Cranes are symbols of:
- Marital fidelity
- Mate and parental devotion
- Vigilance (particularly against enemies or evil)
- Luck
- Intelligence or deep contemplation
- Weather omens, most notably, the change of seasons, especially the arrival of spring, and impending rain.

"Every land where they appear has tales and myths about the cranes, which since ancient times have represented longevity and good fortune, harmony and fidelity."

— Peter Matthiessen in *The Birds of Heaven*

WHAT IS IN A NAME?

Crane (kræn) n. **1.** Any of various large wading birds of the family Gruidae, having a long neck, long legs, and a long bill.

The modern English word crane is derived from Old English *cran* and the Old German *krano*. These in turn derive from an ancestral Indo-European root, *gar, ker,* *"to cry out."* The Cornish word for crane *garan* derives from the Greek geranos.

The Latin word for crane is *grus*. The French word *grue* is derived from the Latin grus. Interestingly, the French grue gives us the English word pedigree, from pied de grue, meaning literally "foot of the crane." The shape of the crane's foot refers to a succession mark made on French genealogy charts. The word congruence stems from the ancient Roman word for cranes *grues* because cranes were attributed with a high degree of cooperative behavior.

CRANE PLACE NAMES

For many years extirpated from the United Kingdom, it is known that the Eurasian Crane *Grus grus* once inhabited northern England, Ireland and Scotland. (Armstrong, 1979). Indeed many English words and place names bear the name *cran:*

Crandell/Crandall: Old English for valley of cranes.
Cranley: Old English for meadow with the cranes.
Cranston: Old English for settlement of cranes.

Crane as an entrée, was listed on an extensive inventory of wild fowl served at elaborate banquets in the Court of King Henry VIII. Eurasian Cranes are now making a slow comeback in England. Once a common sight in days of old, their wetland homes were extensively drained centuries ago for agricultural purposes. In 2007, after an absence of over 400 years, Eurasian Cranes were reportedly nesting in Lakenheath Fen Nature Reserve in Suffolk, England.

The Crane,

The giant with his trumpet-sound

— Geoffrey Chaucer - *Parliament of Fowls,* 1400

CRANE-BERRY

European settlers to North America discovered what Native Americans had known for centuries – cranberries are a good source of nutrition and medicine. The settlers supposedly named the fruit "crane-berry" due to the resemblance of the stem and flower of the plant just before opening, to that of a crane's head and graceful neck. It's more likely, however, that the name cranberry referred to the crane's penchant for eating the berries in watery bogs. Hundreds of years ago, many northern European countries sustained the bogs, the berries, and the cranes — for which this berry is named. The English word derives from the German "Kranbeere." When European marshes were drained, the cranes and the berries they loved disappeared. European immigrants to North America may well have been familiar with the crane-berry (or a similar species) long before arriving on these shores.

"DAMSEL" CRANE

Demoiselle Cranes *Anthropoides virgo* are the smallest and third most abundant crane species. From the French, we have the common name for this dainty (yet feisty!) little crane. Demoiselles were first brought to France from the steppes of Russia and presented at the Court of Louis XVI. Historians tell us that the name was bestowed by the French Queen Marie Antoinette, who was taken with this crane's delicate and maiden-like appearance, hence the name demoiselle, meaning a young maiden of noble birth.

GERANOS

The Greek word for crane geranos gives us the English word for the plant geranium. It is a reference to the geranium's long-beaked seedpod that resembles a crane's bill. In fact, the word cranesbill is the common name for the wild geranium.

THE GREEK ALPHABET

Greek mythology maintains that several letters from the Greek alphabet are taken from the shape of cranes in flight. Around the time of the Trojan War, Palamedes, inspired by watching cranes, supposedly invented four new Greek letters:

$$\Xi \quad \Phi \quad X \quad \Theta$$

This would explain why cranes were sometimes referred to as *Avis Palamedis* (Topsell).

Read More About It:

Graves, Robert. *The White Goddess: a Historical Grammar of Poetic Myth.* New York: Farrar, Straus and Giroux, 1975.

Topsell, Edward, and Ulisse Aldrovandi. *The Fowles of Heaven or History of Birdes.* Austin: University of Texas, 1972.

CRANE LETTERS

It was believed in classical times that the Greek letter Phi in particular resembles a crane in its typical roosting pose on one leg with its head tucked under one wing.

THE FLIGHT OF CRANES

Some Greek scholars attribute the entire Greek alphabet to the flight of cranes. The god Mercury supposedly collected all of the letters from flying cranes. Frequent references to the alphabet and the flight of cranes exist in old texts:

Take but the letter which the crane did make:
From verse, then sense from it, her flight doth take.

— Martiall, 40-108 AD

With wings they write plain letters varying place,
Scribbling in air with quills uncut and wilde.

— Claudianus

EDWARD TOPSELL

Much of what we know about cranes during the classical period comes by way of Edward Topsell (1572-1625). Little is known of Topsell's life other than that he was an English clergyman and naturalist. His interest in zoology appears to have been stimulated by the need to identify the various animals referred to in the Bible. He published his *Historie of Four-footed Beastes* in1607, and *Historie of Serpents* in 1608.

His final manuscript on birds, *The Fowles of Heaven* or *History of Birdes* (1613-14) was never finished. He completed chapters for birds beginning with the letters A, B, and C. The unfinished manuscript was eventually published in 1972 by the University of Texas Press, and is a treasure trove of information on classical beliefs about cranes.

IMITATE THE LETTERS OF THE ALPHABET

Topsell relates Cicero's description of the crane's efficient manner of migration and that their method certainly relates to the alphabet:

Every one layeth or resteth his necke upon the backe of him that flieth next before him. And because the foremost cannot do so, having none upon whome to rest, He turneth aside and commeth behinde, and so layeth his head and necke upon that crane that carried nothinge: And so doth the same that had the next foreplace, every one in his order, after a certeine distance of tyme and place. By this chainginge they imitate the letters of the alphabet in writinge, wherein they are chainged one after another according as the spellinge of the worde requireth.

THE CRANE'S NECK

- The crane's most prominent feature, its neck, produced the verb to crane, or stretch the neck, and is dated to the 18th century.

- Metaphorical use of the word crane for a "machine with a long neck" dates back to the 13th century. Modern cranes are used in the construction trades, while medieval mechanical cranes were used in theatrical productions.

- English historian Edward Topsell mentions a precious stone from ancient times named for the crane's neck called *geranitis*.

- A whimsical motif in some Native American folktales is that of the crane using his neck to span a river in order to provide a "bridge" or escape route for animals fleeing an enemy.

STONY SYMBOLS

Most peculiar of all the stories about cranes are the unusual number of references to cranes and stones in legends and lore. Historian Edward Topsell discusses in the *Fowles of Heaven* Greek theories concerning cranes and stones. The legend below is attributed to Plutarch, but later infiltrates Asian and European mythology.

> Amongst each flock of roosting cranes, there is one individual charged with the safety of the others. The sentinel stands on one foot in shallow water. The elevated foot holds a stone as a safeguard against falling asleep. If the sentinel happens to fall asleep, his relaxation causes him to lose his grip upon the stone. The stone then falls into the water causing a splash that awakens the malingering watchman.

VIGILANCE

The legend of the crane watchman holding a stone explains why in British heraldry, the crane is always depicted holding a stone. This pose signifies vigilance.

Christians believed that a crane on guard duty symbolizes a man's duty to protect himself and his family from the plots of his enemies.

MORE STONE STORIES

Some Greek writers thought that cranes swallowed a heavy stone before migrating. The stone was thought to serve as ballast – to keep the cranes from blowing off course during heavy winds. While Aelianus thought the cranes regurgitated the stone at the end of their journey, Pliny believed that sand was regurgitated after a long migration. The sand would come up as a yellow stone, that when heated turned into gold.

KERPLUNK

Aristophanes believed that cranes held a stone in their claws, and while flying high on migration and uncertain of their course, would let the stone fall. With their sensitive hearing, the crane would listen carefully for a splash or a thud. Based upon the sound they heard, the migrating cranes would be able to ascertain if they were over land or water.

STONY SILENCE

The Greeks believed that the crane's natural inclination was to "clamor" during migration to communicate and keep the flock on course, but cranes were also known to be attacked by eagles during migration. The urge to make noise on their journey, however, might attract the attention of marauding eagles, something the cranes would want to avoid. Some Greek historians believed the birds flew at night, and kept stones in their mouths to stifle their natural urge to make noise to communicate, and thus not attract the attention of eagles.

EGG OR STONE?

We see that tame and domestical cranes do every yere
lay a stone in their nest, among their eggs, making no
choice or election thereof; but take any stone without
difference. It may be doubted whether they would do
the like if they were at liberty.

— Albertus

For a variety of reasons in captivity, breeding cranes are occasionally given "dummy" eggs made of wood or plaster to replace their real eggs. Most cranes readily accept and lovingly sit on the imposter eggs. At the International Crane Foundation in Baraboo, Wisconsin, birds on exhibit have been known to select rocks from their enclosures and place them in their nests to incubate. Their behavior toward the stones is exactly as if they were real eggs.

BONE HEALING STONE

A Tibetan belief is that the Black-necked Crane (Trung-Trung) can identify a special kind of bone-healing stone. If a person breaks a bone, it is possible to heal it by obtaining this very special stone by following the convoluted method described in the Tibetan medicinal manual:

> The person who wishes to obtain the bone-healing stone must quietly creep up to a crane's nest, and wait until the adult bird flies off. When the bird is gone, one must gently paint a black circle on the egg in the nest and then hide a distance away. When the crane returns, it will mistakenly think the eggshell is broken and will then fly off in search of the mystical bone-healing stone to fix the broken egg. When the crane brings the stone back to the nest it can then be taken away.

CRANES AND DEMETER

Cranes are often associated with the goddess Demeter because they are a symbol of the advent of spring and the return of Persephone.

The Greek goddess Demeter is intimately associated with the seasons. Hades, god of the underworld, abducted her daughter Persephone. Angry Demeter laid a curse on the world that caused plants to die, and the land became desolate and infertile. Zeus became alarmed and sought Persephone's return, but, because she had eaten while in the underworld Hades had a claim on her. It was decreed that Persephone would spend four months of each year in the underworld. During these months Demeter grieves her daughter's absence, and withdraws her gifts from the world, creating winter. Persephone's return from Hades brings spring. Cranes are symbolic of the forthcoming season, and Demeter's joy at the return of her beloved daughter.

CRANE DANCE OF THESEUS

In modern day Greece the *Geranos,* or Crane Dance, is modeled on the crane's mating ritual, and is performed by humans as an expression of love. Its origins may have come from a long forgotten solar cult, which in turn had its origins in the legends of Theseus.

On the island of Crete, Theseus slayed the Minotaur of King Minos, ending the annual human sacrifice in the Labyrinth. He rescued seven boys and seven maidens. After his famous deed, Theseus and his men danced the Geranos to honor the sun. The serpentine movements were thought to imitate the complicated maze, but later evolved as an emulation of dancing cranes by the inhabitants of Delos who continued performing the dance.

GERANIA

There is a mountain near Corinth called Gerania (from geranos, the Greek word for crane). It is said that during a terrible flood the inhabitants of the area followed the calls of cranes to higher ground and were saved from drowning.

An alternate version of this story is that of Megarus, son of Zeus, who escaped Deucalion's flood by swimming to the top of Mount Gerania. He was guided to safety by the cries of cranes.

CRANES AND SNAKES

In Thessaly (central Greece) cranes were admired for killing and eating snakes. Without the cranes' habit of eating the snakes, people believed the area would have been uninhabitable for humans. For this reason, the law protected the beneficial cranes.

As killers of snakes, cranes in Christianity are symbolic as enemies of Satan.

THE CRANES OF IBYCUS

In ancient Greece the famous story of the *Cranes of Ibycus* possibly demonstrates the origins of the belief that murderers will always be found out. According to this legend, the poet named Ibycus was on his way to the chariot races in Corinth when he was robbed and killed by a band of thieves around 550 B.C. As Ibycus lay dying, he looked above and saw a group of cranes flying overhead. Ibycus called upon them to expose his murderers.

> *"Take up my cause, ye cranes," he said,*
> *"since no voice but yours answers to my cry."*

Shortly after the incident, while one of the thieves was in the streets of Corinth, he saw the cranes flying overhead. His shock at seeing the same cranes caused him to cry out loudly,

> *"Behold the cranes of Ibycus!"*

Suspicious of this strange outburst, friends of Ibycus investigated and the murderers ultimately confessed their crime.

CRANES AND PYGMIES

An unusual legend that occurs in the lore of several cultures is that of the feud between cranes and pygmies. First recorded by the Greeks, the fundamental motif even appears in early compilations of native North American folklore, where the small people are known as the Tsundige'wi.

> In the autumn, cranes were thought to migrate to the land of the pygmies, which was believed to exist in India, Egypt or Ethiopia. Their arrival always led to bloody warfare or geranomachian (from the Greek word for crane, geranos) between the cranes and pygmies. The pygmies tried to defend their crops from the ravages of the cranes, but were usually defeated.

The Iliad compares the noisy Trojan warriors to shrieking cranes descending upon the silent Pygmy soldiers in the following passage:

> The Trojans came with cries and the din of war like wildfowl when the long hoarse cries of cranes sweep on against the sky and the great formations flee from winter's grim ungodly storms, flying in force, shrieking south to the ocean gulfs, speeding blood and death to the Pygmy warriors, launching at daybreak savage battle down upon their heads.

> The clamour of cranes goes high to the heavens, when the cranes escape the winter time and the rains unceasing and clamorously wing their way to streaming Okeanos, bringing the Pygmaioi men bloodshed and destruction: at daybreak they bring on the baleful battle against them."

> – Iliad 3.3

GERANOMACHIAN

"This tribe (the Pygmaioi) Homer has also recorded as being beset by cranes. It is reported that in springtime their entire band, mounted on the backs of rams and she-goats and armed with arrows, goes in a body down to the sea and eats the cranes' eggs and chickens, and that this outing occupies three months; and that otherwise they could not protect themselves against the flocks of cranes; and that their houses are made of mud and feathers and egg-shells."

– Pliny Natural History 7.26

"Like Thrakian cranes, when they fly from the scourge of winter and floods of stormy rain to throw their great flocks against the heads of Pygmaioi (Pygmies) round the waters of Tethys, and when with sharp beaks they have destroyed that weak and helpless race, they wing their way like a cloud over the horn of Okeanos."

– Dionysiaca 14.332

THE TSUNDIGE'WI

Once, some young Cherokee men journeyed south to see the world. They came upon a tribe of little people called Tsundige'wi, with strange little bodies and only a few feet tall. The Tsundige'wi lived in nests covered with dried grass. Because they were so small, the little people lived in constant fear from the wild birds that came in great flocks from the south to attack them. They told the Cherokee they did not know how to fight the birds. The Cherokee showed them how to hit the birds with strong sticks.

When the birds finally arrived, the little men ran to their nests. The birds stuck their long bills in to pull them out and eat them. This time, however, the Tsundige'wi used their sticks and drove the birds away.

They thanked the Cherokee for their help and gave them their best hospitality. The Cherokee heard later that the birds came again several times, but that the Tsundige'wi were able to drive them off with their sticks. The sticks worked until a flock of Sandhill Cranes arrived. They were so tall that the little men could not reach up to strike them on the neck, and so at last the cranes killed them all and that is why there are no more Tsundige'wi.

– *Myths of the Cherokee*, James Mooney, 1900

GERANA, QUEEN OF THE PYGMIES

If cranes are the sworn enemies of the Pygmies, why then would their queen bear the name representing cranes? Gerana derives from geranos the Greek word for crane. This puzzle is explained in Ovid's *Metamorphoses:*

> "The Pygmy matron's doom, her pitiable doom, when Hera won the contest and transformed her to a crane and made her fight her folk, her kith and kin."   – *Metamorphoses* 6.90

The goddess Hera became furious with the Pygmy queen Gerana. Gerana apparently boasted that she was lovelier than the immortal Hera. Her vanity cost her dearly as Hera changed her into a crane, the bitter enemy of her people. When her subjects saw her, they mistook her for a real crane, attacked, and killed her.

An alternate version of Gerana's story:

> Gerana, queen of the Pygmies, married Nikodamos, and the couple had a son together named Mopsos. Pygmies, like cranes, were known to be devoted parents. The goddess Hera, hearing of Gerana's great beauty, turned Gerana into a crane as a punishment for her conceit, because the cranes were the enemy of her people. From the time she was turned into a bird, Gerana was distraught over losing her baby, and was determined to get Mopsos back. She swooped down out of the sky and grabbed him with her beak. Gerana attempted to flee with her baby in her beak, but her fellow pygmies, not realizing it was their queen, thought that the bird was trying to abduct Mopsos. They grabbed their sticks and drove Gerana away.

CRANE CONSTELLATION

Grus the crane is a little constellation of the southern hemisphere near Indus and Phoenix. It lies below Piscis Austrinus, and is believed to have been a part of that constellation. Grus was named in the 1603 star atlas, *Uranometria*, of Johann Bayer.

Horapollo of Alexandria (AD 400) states that the crane was the symbol for astronomers, or star-observers in Egypt, probably due to its ability to fly extremely high aloft. Horapollo believed that cranes flew at high altitudes in order to inspect the clouds for rain. Ancients also noted that during their dramatic unison call, crane pairs lift their heads to the sky to trumpet to the heavens.

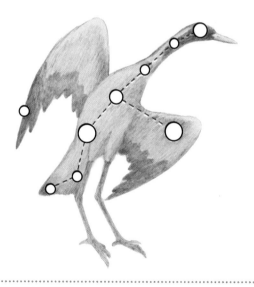

WEATHER VANE CRANE

Birds and animals in the natural world were often seen as indicators of impending weather change. Cranes were considered a forecaster for rain.

> *Marke and beholde when cranes from cloudes ethereall,*
> *Do jangle loude,*
> *Then tempests showres doe call.*

Since ancient times, the distinctive bugling of cranes migrating signaled to farmers the commencement of important agricultural practices.

The Greek poet Hesiod counseled farmers:

> *Take heed what time thou hearest the voice of the crane*
> *Who, year by year, from out the clouds on high*
> *Clangs shrilly, for her voice bringeth the sign*
> *For ploughing.*

> *When cranes come hither tis springe and sowing tyme,*
> *They feede on grayne uncouvered which they find.*

EGYPTIANS AND CRANES

Egyptian art holds many representations of the Eurasian Crane *Grus grus* and occasional representations of the Demoiselle *Anthropoides virgo*. Depictions are rarely of wild cranes, but rather, of cranes kept in captivity. The cranes were kept in poultry yards with other species of fowl, mainly to be fattened and eaten, but occasionally were kept as pets by wealthy Egyptians. The Mastaba (tomb) of Atet from the IV Dynasty depicts Atet's son playing with his pets, one of which is a crane. Cranes were most commonly shown in these domestic situations or in funeral processions on tomb and temple walls, such as the depiction of the offering of Demoiselle Cranes for Queen Hatshepsut. A striking relief of a flock of mixed species cranes is located at the Mastaba of Ti at Saqqara.

According to Egyptian legend, a two-headed crane was once seen flying over the Nile, announcing an age of joy and prosperity.

HOODWINKED

Plutarch relates the practice of sewing shut the eyelids of captive cranes. This method was supposed to calm the wild birds so they could be fattened in captivity. This practice is the origin of the phrase, *to be hoodwinked.* While the modern day meaning of hoodwink is *to take in by deceptive means,* the archaic meaning is *to blindfold* or *conceal.*

AESOP'S FABLES AND THE JATAKA

Fables were a popular method to teach morals and values to children. Aesop's fables employ birds and animals to teach these morals. There are seven crane fables or references to cranes in the popular collection known as *Aesop's Fables.* Not much is known about Aesop. One theory is that he was an African slave living in ancient Greece who became a popular storyteller.

The *Jataka* is a large body of folklore and mythic literature associated with the Buddhist tradition in India. *The Wolf and the Crane* story from Aesop is similar to *The Lion and the Crane* story from the Jataka. The tales from the Jataka were eventually codified, probably in the third century, A.D., although the oral tradition dates back much earlier. After their codification, the stories were translated into many languages including Persian, Greek, Latin and Hebrew. Some historians believe they form the basis for *Aesop's Fables* and *The Arabian Nights.* There is no doubt though, that the Jataka tales disseminated from India and became infused in the world's folk literature.

AESOP'S FABLES:
THE WOLF AND THE CRANE

A Wolf was hungrily consuming his dinner when suddenly a sharp bone became uncomfortably stuck in his throat. Try as he might, he could not swallow or dislodge it. The pain frightened him and he began to cry out loudly for help. Alas, all the animals he begged for help refused him. They feared the wolf. Finally, a Crane walked past and told the Wolf that he could easily remove the offending bone. The Wolf promised the Crane a handsome reward to complete the task. The Crane told the Wolf to open his mouth wide. He then stuck his head in past the sharp teeth that could easily decapitate him. The Crane's strong beak effortlessly pulled the bone free and the Wolf was instantly relieved of his painful predicament.

"I will take my payment now," said the Crane. The Wolf's teeth gleamed as he laughed, "Be happy that you are still alive Crane. You put your head inside my mouth and still live. That should be reward enough for your silliness."

Moral of the story:

A villain will never reward you for a job well done – a safe escape is your reward for having the bad judgment to consort with the wicked.

AESOP'S FABLES:
THE FARMER AND THE CRANES

Some cranes made their feeding grounds on some farmlands newly sown with wheat. For a long time the farmer, brandishing an empty sling, chased them away by the terror he inspired; but when the birds found that the sling was only swung in the air, they ceased to take any notice of it and would not move. The farmer, on seeing this, charged his sling with stones, and killed a great number. The remaining birds at once forsook his fields, crying to each other, "It is time for us to be off. This man is no longer content to scare us, but begins to show us in earnest what he can do."

If words suffice not, blows must follow.

AESOP'S FABLES:
THE STORK AND THE CRANES

The cranes were making trouble for the farmer by eating the seed he had scattered on his field. There was a stork there also who associated with the cranes and lived together with them although he never ate the newly planted seeds. When the farmer was fed up with the damage being done to his crops, he prepared a trap and captured the stork along with the cranes. Moral of the story: If you consort with wicked people, you will receive the same punishment they do as you are guilty by association.

While these are ancient fables, crop depredation by cranes and other birds is still a problem today. When cranes or other wildlife consume the crops of farmers who depend on the crops for survival, conflict arises. The International Crane Foundation is working with farmers around the world to find ways to reduce damage without harming wildlife.

AESOP'S FABLES:
THE GEESE AND THE CRANES

The Geese and the Cranes were feeding in the same meadow, when a bird catcher came to ensnare them in his nets. The Cranes, being light of wing, fled away at his approach; while the Geese, being slower of flight and heavier in their bodies, were captured.

AESOP'S FABLES:
THE PEACOCK AND THE CRANE

A peacock spreading his gorgeous tail mocked a crane that was passing by. The peacock ridiculed the crane's boring plumage proclaiming, "I am dressed like a king, in gold and purple and all the colors of the rainbow, while you are drab and have not a bit of color on your wings."

"True," replied the Crane; "but I fly high through the clouds to the heights of heaven and lift up my voice to the stars, while you strut below among the common birds of the manure pile."

Fine feathers don't make fine birds.

AESOP'S FABLES:
THE FOX AND THE CRANE

Fox invited Crane to supper. When Crane arrived he was served a plain soup on a flat stone dish. Crane became frustrated quickly because he was unable to get the soup into his bill. Fox was greatly amused at Crane's inability to eat the soup, and was happy to have all the soup for himself.

Crane, in turn, invited Fox to have dinner with him. Crane placed before Fox a tall jug with a long narrow mouth filled with soup. Fox was unable to figure out how to get a taste of the soup as he couldn't get his snout inside. Crane, on the other hand, was leisurely enjoying the soup with his long beak. Crane thought this was a good response to Fox's dreadful hospitality.

AESOP'S FABLES:
THE CRANE AND THE CROW

A crane and a crow had made a mutual promise to help each other. The crane was to protect the crow from other birds, while the crow would use her powers of prophecy to warn the crane about future events. The two birds liked to go to a certain farmer's field to eat the tasty crops there. When the farmer saw what was happening to his field, he was angry and told his son to give him a rock. The crow alerted the crane, and they wisely made their escape. On another occasion, the crow again heard the farmer asking for a rock and warned the crane so that the crane could escape.

After a while, the farmer realized the crow was able to warn the crane. He told his son to give him a rock when he said, "give me some bread." When the crow and the crane were next in the field, the farmer told his son to give him some bread, so the boy gave him a rock. The farmer threw the stone at the crane and broke both his legs. The injured crane said to the crow, "What has become of your god-given talent of prophecy? Why didn't you warn me that this was going to happen?" The crow then said to the crane, "In this case it is not my understanding that is at fault. These people are very clever, they say one thing and do another!"

VALMIKI'S CURSE

The Sarus or Sárás Crane, *Grus antigone* is the world's tallest flying bird. Although their historic range was once much larger, they now occur in northern and central India, southeastern Pakistan, southern Myanmar, Cambodia, southern Laos, Vietnam, and northern Australia. The word Sárás derives from the Sanskrit *sárása*, which means to belong to or come from a lake or pond. They are the official state bird of Uttar Pradesh, India and are associated with Hindu mythology including a role in the genesis of the epic poem, *The Ramayana*.

Valmiki walked to the banks of the river for a bath. There he became entranced by the sight of a pair of courting cranes. Suddenly, a hunter appeared and shot the male bird dead with an arrow while the bird was distracted by its mate. Witnessing this shocking event and hearing the mournful cries of the bereaved female crane, Valmiki cursed the hunter on the spot. Witnessing this grief at the death of a life partner inspired what happened next to Valmiki. To his astonishment, the curse emerged from his mouth as a perfectly formed metrical verse, suitable for accompaniment with musical instruments. Valmiki returned to his ashram, pondering this strange event. Lord Brahma appeared and told him that it was he himself who had enabled him to transform the powerful emotion of grief into a new means of verbal expression.

Lord Brahma also told Valmiki that the purpose of this divine inspiration was to enable him to render the tale of Lord Rama into a great epic poem that would be both morally uplifting and very entertaining. Valmiki then composed *The Ramayana*, a massive epic in seven books (kandas) containing over 50,000 lines of Sanskrit verse.

These strong feelings of deep regard for the intense pair bond of the Sarus Crane still exist among rural people of India where Sarus Cranes occur.

HAPPY HITCHHIKERS?

There is a quirky mystique that cranes sometimes convey smaller birds on their backs or under their wings. American naturalist Ernest Ingersoll, writing in 1923 about bird legends relates, "Sir Samuel Baker encountered in Abyssinia [Ethiopia] bands of cranes walking about in search of grasshoppers, every crane carrying on its back one or more small flycatchers that from time to time would fly down, seize an insect in the grass, and then return to a crane's shoulders." The famous naturalist Johann Gmelin (1748-1804) was assured by Siberian Tartars (Turkic people of Eastern Europe) that cranes carried corncrakes *Crex crex* south on their backs.

An article entitled, "The Singular Methods of Travel the Wagtail Adopts to Cross the Mediterranean Sea" appeared in the journal *Nature* in 1881. In the article, a European bird enthusiast reported that it was common knowledge of the locals on the island of Crete that the wagtails arrive there from Europe riding with Eurasian Cranes. Later, in Egypt, the same man saw wagtails near the pyramids, and inquired of an old man how the birds could possibly make such a long journey. The old man replied, "These small birds are borne over the sea by the larger ones...Every child among us knows that."

Indigenous people of the far northern areas of North America claim that the "little birds" fly up to the cranes and hide in a hollow place under the cranes' wings. This occurs in the autumn on the tundra as the cranes are preparing to leave on migration. They then carry the little birds along with them on their journey southward.

THE CRANE'S BACK

The Crow people of Montana believed that Sandhill Cranes carried small birds (likely a small grebe) on their backs. The name for the bird, *napite-shu-utl* literally means, "crane's back," and was a highly prized bird when captured. Crow warriors carried small bone whistles into battle. The origin of the whistle and its connection to the crane is related in an 1881 issue of *Forest and Stream*. J.C. Merrill of Fort Custer, Montana writes:

> About ten or fifteen percent of cranes are accompanied by the 'craneback' which, as the crane rises from the ground, flutters up and settles on the back between the wings, remaining there until the crane alights... At these times the small bird is said to keep up a constant chattering whistle, which is the origin of the custom of the Crow warriors going out to battle, each with a small bone whistle in his mouth; this is continually blown, imitating the notes of the 'crane's-back,' and, as they believe, preserves their ponies and themselves from wounds, so that in case of defeat they may be safely carried away as is the napite-shu-utl. The Cree Indians are said to observe the same habit in the white crane [Whooping Crane].

NORTH AMERICA

Two species of cranes occur in North America — the most abundant species, the Sandhill Crane, and the rarest, the Whooping Crane. As early as 900 AD, cranes appear in pictographs, petroglyphs, and ceramics in North America. Pictographs and cave paintings of cranes are numerous among the Pueblo. Sandhill Cranes and probably Whooping Cranes migrated through southwestern United States, and have been used as clan symbols, in rituals and on various handicrafts such as bowls. Crane bones have been found in New Mexico in the form of tools, beads and whistles. Navajos used Sandhill Crane bills and heads as a medicine pouch and also made medicine spoons from the beak. Whooping Cranes were once referred to in northern Mexico as *viejos del agua* or "old men of the water."

Meriwether Lewis of the famous expedition made this entry about encountering Whooping Cranes in his journal,

> *"We killed two geese and saw some cranes, the largest*
> *bird of that kind common to the Missouri and Mississippi*
> *perfectly white except the large feathers on the first joint*
> *of the wing, which are black."*
>
> — Journal Entry, April 11, 1805

TOTEMS

The following North American tribes are known to have cranes as totems. Totems are usually plants or animals that are honored by a person or group of people. Totems are sometimes considered the ancestor of the group and are portrayed as a symbol or protector. Totems can be depicted on masks, the body, on poles or other artwork.

Algonkin Tribes on the Atlantic
- Delawares or Lenapes
- Mohicans
- Abenakis (Maine)

Mississippi Algonkin Tribes
- Menomonis
- Ojibwes

Pueblo Tribes
- Hopi
- Zunis

Northwest Indians
- Tsimshian
- Omahas

AZTECA: THE CRANE PEOPLE

The Aztecs were a Mesoamerican people of Mexico who rose from humble origins to create a vibrant culture and eventually established what is today known as Mexico City. The Aztecs were conquered by Spanish conquistadors in the 16th century.

It is generally believed by historians that, in their early days, the Aztecs were named the "People of the Crane" by their neighbors, the Tecpanecs (a stronger tribe than the Aztecs at that time), because they lived in a marshy area near the cranes. The modern English word Aztec derives from the Spanish Aztecâ, which derives from the Nahuatl word *Aztecatl,* which means "people from Aztlan." Aztlan is the ancestral home of the Aztecs before their migration in A.D. 1168 to Anahuac in the Valley of Mexico.

The probable etymology of Aztlan is "near the cranes," from *azta* for cranes, and *tlan* for near or "the place of." Aztlan is sometimes translated as "place of whiteness." The Aztecs rarely used the word Aztecatl to describe themselves. Their self-name was the *Mexica.* The location of Aztlan is believed to be in what is now the north of Mexico or possibly the southwest region of the United States. Interestingly, some biologists believe that the historic range of the conspicuous and very white Whooping Crane, *Grus americana* included this area of northern Mexico, and thus the interpretation of Aztlan as *the Place of the Cranes* is not at all implausible. The existence of Aztlan, a place far to the north, was reported by Spanish conquerors as a utopian paradise, free of disease and full of riches. These stories stimulated expeditions into northern Mexico and southwestern United States.

HOW COYOTE STOLE FIRE FROM CRANE
Or Why Chipmunks Have Stripes

For countless years humans have created stories to explain things in the natural world. The "How" and "Why" stories are some of the most endearing stories about cranes.

> Before there were people, no one had fire except Crane, king of the birds. He and his family kept the fire to themselves and guarded it carefully. One day, all the animals got together and decided to steal fire from Crane. They sent Coyote to Crane's camp for dinner. He ate with the Cranes and after dinner he suggested they dance around the fire. Everyone knows cranes love to dance. Coyote wore a long feather headdress and joined in the dancing. He intentionally danced closer and closer to the fire until his feathers swayed into the flames and ignited. As soon as they were on fire, he ran as fast as he could out of the camp. The Cranes, realizing Coyote's cunning ploy to steal their fire, took to the skies and pursued overhead yelling, "Stop Thief!"
>
> Just as Coyote was tiring, he ran into Chipmunk, who quickly took the burning feathers and ran away. But Chipmunk, fearing the loss of this treasure, held the smoldering mass too tightly and burned black streaks on his body, which he still has to this day. The Cranes eventually gave up and flew home. Coyote and Chipmunk carried fire to all the other animals so they could be warm in winter.

WHY CRANE FLIES WITH OUTSTRETCHED LEGS
Also known as Theft of Pine Nuts

There are many versions of this Shoshone tale.

Crow and Crane argued over pine nuts. Crow won the pine nuts from Crane by cheating at a ball game. (Ball games between animals or animals and birds are a recurring theme in many North American stories.) Angrily Crane chased Crow and killed him. Crow, however, was not really dead. He put the pine nuts in his broken off leg and the broken leg ran off with the pine nuts.

Crane, unable to find the stolen pine nuts, was still hungry and spied a camp in the mountains and could smell roasting pine nuts. The aroma was irresistible. Crane joined the group in the mountains, but they only gave him bad, wormy pine nuts. When Crane got up to leave, an old woman hit him with a large stick. She was afraid he would fly off with the good pine nuts. She knocked off all his tail feathers with the stick.

This is why today cranes have very few tail feathers and Crane must make a tail out of his legs by letting them trail behind him like a tail. Meanwhile, Crow retrieved the broken leg full of pine nuts, but he choked on his ill-gotten pine nuts while gobbling them down. They were permanently stuck in his throat, which is why still today Crow's call is "caw, caw."

SANDHILL CRANES:
A PUEBLO TALE

Once, long ago, a flock of cranes lived up in the clouds. They lived quite happily in the sky, drinking water from the clouds and even building nests there. One day they decided to go down to earth and drink and eat of the fish in the rivers. At the first river, they ate all the fish and frogs and drank all the water. They moved on to a second and third river, and did the same again. Finally, they went to the Rio Grande, but were unable to eat and drink all that was there, no matter how hard they tried. "This is a mighty and great river," their leader said, "we shall make our home here and prosper."

CRANES AND CLOWNS

In the Tewa Society (their homelands are on or near the Rio Grande in New Mexico north of Santa Fe), Crane Old Man guards Kachina dancers and Clowns. Clowns are powerful yet humorous figures similar to tricksters or a court jester. They have license to poke fun at behavior within their society. The purpose of their sometimes outrageous parodies are meant to demonstrate acceptable social behavior. In the Zuni Society, all Clowns are chosen from the Crane Clan, and only they may use Sandhill Crane feathers in secret rituals.

BLUE EYED CRANES

The endangered Whooping Crane's northern breeding range is in the upper reaches of the North American continent. Whoopers now spend summers in Canada's Wood Buffalo National Park, Northwest Territories, so it naturally follows that there might be stories about them in the lore of the natives of that area. There are several variations of a story about how Crane came by his blue eyes.

In fact, most adult Whooping Cranes have eyes that range in color from yellow or gold, to red. Only the Siberian and Whooping Cranes have chicks with blue eyes. Whooping Cranes are born with blue eyes that change color as they grow older. At about three months, their eyes are a beautiful aquamarine color. At about six months, their eyes are bright gold. The Canadian tale speaks specifically of a Whooping Crane, while a Yup'ik story speaks generically of a crane. Yup'ik is the self-name for those of western coastal Alaska.

WHY THE WHOOPING CRANE HAS BLUE EYES

Every year in the far northern lands, arrived a bird named the Whooping Crane. Whooper flew high in the sky, looking far and wide for danger before landing after his long journey. After such a flight Crane wished to refresh himself and landed by a pond to wash up. He plunged his head in the cool water, while repeatedly lifting his head to look around for danger. His eyes became very weary of being dunked in and out of the cold water.

Crane decided to give his eyes a rest and removed them from the sockets. He carefully set them on a rock to watch for predators so he could wash in peace. He placed them on two different rocks so they could watch in two directions. A clever fox sat nearby hiding behind a blueberry bush watching Whooper as he placed his eyes on the rocks. The mischievous fox crept in from the direction from which the eyes could not see. He snatched Whooper's eyes and replaced them with blueberries from the nearby bush. Chuckling, the fox ran away with Whooper's eyes. Unaware that his eyes had disappeared, Crane finished his bath and reached for his eyes. He grasped the blueberries and replaced them in the sockets not realizing that he now had blueberries for eyes! From that time on, Whooper's blue eyes were very attractive to the female cranes and consequently he had the most offspring, which is why today all the whooping crane chicks have blue eyes.

In the Yup'ik legend, Crane's eyes float away with the tide while he is bathing, and Crane searches desperately for a replacement. He tries all sorts of different berries, but they make the world look too red, or pink or spotted. Finally, Crane tries blueberries and is quite satisfied with the way the world appears.

CRANE AND COYOTE: A WINTU TALE

Similar to the "eye motif" story of *How Crane Got Blue Eyes* is the story of Sedit (Coyote) and Torraharsh (Sandhill Crane) of the Wintu people of northern California.

Crane and Coyote decided to leave Shasta Valley and travel south together to see the sights and seek their fortune. They met many friends along the way, but kept heading south to the big valley. Finally they reached the big valley where there were many new people playing the grass game and gambling. Crane and Coyote gambled too and eventually won everyone's beads. They stayed for the winter. After some time passed, two gopher brothers came to the valley and wanted to gamble. They gambled and gambled and won everything that Crane and Coyote had won from others. They even won a most valuable possession – their eyes!

Just before Crane and Coyote removed their eyes from their sockets to give to the gopher brothers, Coyote discovered that the gophers were cheating by having one gopher underground and reporting back to the gopher above ground. Unfortunately for Crane and Coyote this discovery came too late... they had already lost everything including their eyesight.

The morning after losing their eyes they set out for home, blind leading the blind. They were downtrodden, hungry and helpless. After marching miserably for many hours, Crane heard the sound of water and caught a fish. Crane removed the fish's eyes and put them in his own empty sockets. Crane used his new eyesight to catch another fish for Coyote.

With eyes, they could now see to make their way home again.

To this day cranes and coyotes are the sworn enemies of gophers and will attack them any chance they have, Crane with his long bill and Coyote with his long teeth.

WHY CRANE HAS LONG LEGS AND A RED CROWN: A CREE TALE

Once, long ago, Rabbit thought it would be nice to go to the moon to have a look around. But how would he get there? He would need the help of someone who could fly. Rabbit asked all the large birds, one at a time, to fly him to the moon. He asked Hawk. He asked Eagle. Hawk was too busy, and Eagle said he couldn't fly that high. Overhearing the conversation, Crane offered to fly Rabbit to the moon. Crane knew he could fly higher than the other birds. Rabbit held tightly to Crane's legs and up they went toward the moon. Rabbit became heavier and heavier to Crane as he flew upward and his legs began to stretch longer and longer. The physical effort to fly Rabbit to the moon was tiring Crane and his head turned bright red. Finally, they reached the moon and were rewarded with a delightful view of earth.

To this day, Crane has long legs from the weight of carrying Rabbit such a distance and a red crown from the extreme physical effort to fly him to the moon.

WISAHKECAHK
How Crane Got Long Legs and Why There are Muskegs

A story similar to "How Crane Got His Long Legs," is that of the Cree Trickster Wisahkecahk. The Cree of Canada are part of the First Nation group. Tricksters are powerful spirit beings who love to play tricks on people and animals. The Trickster is often good-natured. Sometimes the Trickster is a raven (British Columbia), but Wisahkecahk is in human form. The "muskegs" referred to in the story are swamps or bogs in the Muskeg Region of northern Canada. The word muskeg originates from the Cree language. This Cree story tells the tale of Wisahkecahk and his attempt to go to the moon.

Wisahkecahk wishes to go to the moon, and convinces Crane to fly him there. On the trip, Wisahkecahk clings to Crane's legs and by the time they reach the moon's surface Crane's legs have stretched to a great length. Crane deposits Wisahkecahk on the moon and returns home. Wisahkecahk thinks he will remain on the moon because the view of earth is wonderful, but unexpectedly the moon begins to shrink and eventually disappears. Wisahkecahk naturally begins to fall back to earth. Luckily though, Wisahkecahk created the things on earth and has a great knowledge of the earth's surface. He wants to fall in a soft spot to avoid injury, and so lands in soft mud. Wisahkecahk, despite being saved by the mud, becomes enraged at being so dirty. He curses the mud as a wasteland and calls it muskeg. Wisahkecahk tells the muskeg that it will have no value for humans.

HOW RAVEN FOOLED SEAGULL AND CRANE: A TLINGIT TALE

Raven is a Trickster in Tlingit stories (Southeastern Alaska).

Once, long ago, Raven strolled along the beach looking hungrily at the water that was teeming with tasty fish. He was ravenous and dearly loved to eat fish, but he was no fisherman. He must use his clever mind to figure a way to get some fish. As he was thinking, he spied Crane in the water a short distance away. Crane was easily catching fish for his dinner. He also saw Seagull sitting on a rock with a protruding gullet full of fish. Oh, how lovely it would be to have those fish inside Seagull's gullet.

He walked over to Crane and said hello, and then walked over to Seagull. After saying hello to Seagull he walked back to Crane and spoke. "Because I am your friend, I'm going to tell you what Seagull just said about you. He said you are an awkward, ugly big bird with no grace."

That said, Raven strolled back to Seagull and spoke. "Because I am your friend, I'm going to tell you what Crane just said about you. He called you bad names and said that your grandmother was a witch." Raven continued going back and forth provoking each bird, while he himself looked like a sympathetic friend. Finally, with coaxing from Raven, Seagull launched an offensive on Crane. Crane, thinking he needed to defend himself from the aggressive Seagull, kicked at Seagull's bulging gullet. Raven had already told Crane this was Seagull's weakest spot.

To Raven's delight, all the fish that Seagull had swallowed burst forth. Raven, who had been waiting for just this turn of events, quickly scooped up all the fish and flew away. Seagull and Crane realized immediately that Raven had deceived them and they stopped fighting. To this day, it is said that all the Tlingit people understand what is meant by the saying, "Perhaps Raven is carrying tales to Crane and Seagull."

THE CRANE AND THE SWAN:
AN INUIT TALE

Swan was sitting at the edge of a lake when Crane came dancing past. Swan suggested they spend some time together. Crane thought this a good idea and suggested they dance together. Swan replied that he was a terrible dancer, but noticed that they both had long necks. Swan suggested they play a game to see who had the strongest neck. Crane agreed and they entwined their necks and began to pull. Crane's neck was proving to be much stronger than Swan's neck. The weakened Swan fell backward. Crane proclaimed himself the winner because he had a strong well-built neck, while Swan's neck was made of nothing but pretty feathers!

CIRCLING CRANES:
AN INUIT STORY FROM THE BERING SEA

Once, long ago, at the end of summer, the cranes were ready to fly south. The cranes gathered into a large flock and circled above the ground when they saw a beautiful girl alone outside the village. The cranes circled above her and then came down and lifted her onto their wings. Some of the birds circled below her so that she wouldn't fall and the clamoring sound of the flock drowned out her calls for help. They carried her off never to be seen again.

To this day, it is believed that cranes circle slowly above, calling out loudly, just before flying off.

ECHO-MAKER:
AN ANISHINABE OJIBWE STORY

The Ojibwe are the third-largest group of Native Americans in the United States, ranging in many different bands across the northern U.S. and Canada. Their self-name is the Anishinabe, or "original people." The Crane Clan is one of five founding clans including Bear, Catfish, Loon and Marten. The crane (ajigaak) is well known for his resounding call, and thus the crane totem represents the echo-maker or a well-spoken leader of the clan. The Anishinabe believe that the social relations of animals can be models for human behavior. A leader should learn to lead from the crane who, though often silent, is always listening. When the crane does finally speak up it is with a distinctive voice, and when the crane calls, all listen.

An origin story from the Great Lakes explains how the Crane Clan came into existence on the shores of Lake Superior.

> The Great Spirit sent two cranes to earth. The cranes were instructed by the Great Spirit to find a suitable place to live. When they found this place, they should wait with their wings folded, for a great change to come over them.

> The cranes flew to earth through the clouds and searched for their new home. First they visited the vast prairies, and tasted buffalo meat. The meat was good, but the cranes did not believe the buffalo would last all year long. Next, they visited the forest, where they tasted the meat of deer and elk. This too was good, but the hunting was very hard work.

Finally, the cranes flew north to the Great Lakes. At the lake the white men call Lake Superior the cranes found an abundance of tasty fish. The cranes were pleased that the fish were so plentiful and easy to catch. "There will never be a shortage of food here!"

They decided to make this their permanent home. The cranes then did as instructed by the Great Spirit and flew to a hill above the water. They waited with their wings folded tightly to their bodies, and their heads tucked in. Suddenly, they were transformed into a man and woman.

The Crane Clan believes they are descended from these two cranes sent to earth by the Great Spirit.

WHY CRANE LEADS BIRDS SOUTH
Or, Ball Game Between the Birds and Animals

There are Creek, Muskogee, Ojibwe, and Cherokee versions of this story, that attempt to explain the great mystery of why some birds fly south every winter. In this tale, Crane is portrayed as the king of the birds.

In order to resolve an argument about strength and courage, the leader of the animals, Bear, and the leader of the birds, Crane, decided to play a ball game (a form of Lacrosse) to determine the winner. The animals and birds divided up into their respective teams, but Bat was left out because she didn't walk upon the earth like animals, nor did she lay eggs like the birds. Finally, because she had teeth, she was accepted as an animal and joined their team. They played and played the ball game all day, but alas, with no clear winner. Finally night fell, and as soon as it was dark, Bat had a tremendous advantage with her superior night-flying abilities. She easily won the game for the animals. As the victorious player, Bat chose the birds' punishment. She decreed that the birds would have to leave the area for half of every year. This is why still today Bat is an animal and why cranes lead the other birds south every year.

WHY SANDHILL CRANE'S FEATHERS ARE BROWN: AN ASSINIBOIN TALE

The Assiniboin speak a Siouan dialect, although the name by which they are popularly known is Algonquian and means "those who cook with stones." They once lived in what is now northern Minnesota and were part of the Yanktonai Sioux, but split off from that tribe and moved to Manitoba and Saskatchewan sometime in the 1600s. Lewis & Clark encountered an Assiniboin Chief named Chechank (Old Crane) in 1804.

Once, long ago, Crane, who was busy with other things, laid her egg very late in the season. All the other birds had already hatched their chicks. Crane realized her egg was so late that the chick would never be able to fly south with her. She worried what to do. Finally when it was time for her to migrate, she asked Otter to care for her chick over the winter. Otter said he would oblige Crane and took her little chick home.

Later, Otter went out to look for food. He was shivering from the cold and was gone a long while. While Otter was out, Osni (cold weather) came and stole Little Crane and took him to his lodge. Osni forced Little Crane to serve him all winter long. Little Crane tended to the fire day and night with his long beak. Soot and ashes from the fire slowly turned his fair beak an ashy gray color. He fanned the flames of Osni's fire with his wings. Eventually his wings were scorched by the fire and turned a drab brown color.

When spring came, Little Crane went outside and called desperately for his mother, "Please help me Mother." Otter heard Little Crane's plea and enlisted the help of Thunder and Lightning to help him rescue Little Crane. Osni refused to give up Little Crane, who he claimed was his grandson. Lightning and Thunder struck Osni, who fell to the ground. At that moment, Crane appeared and thanked Thunder, Lightning, and Otter for saving her son. Crane made a feast for Thunder and Lightning. At the feast Crane said, "I will give you a gift Otter for saving my son. You will no longer feel the cold in the winter. You may play, or swim or hunt in the deep snow or cold water, but you will not feel the least bit cold." And to this day, you can see that Sandhill Cranes have brown feathers, dark beaks, and otters love to romp in the snow and revel in cold weather.

THE STORY OF THE PET CRANE: A SIOUX TALE

A great hunter and his family lived in a secluded place away from the village where the hunting was good. One day the eldest son found an orphaned crane chick when he was out hunting. He took it home to keep as a pet. The crane grew up with the other children and became a beloved member of the family. Eventually there came a time when the hunting was poor and the family was starving. The pet crane went out hunting and brought back meat for the starving family. It was dark, when the mother was cooking the meat. As she stared at the reflection on the cooking pot, she spied an enemy war party outside their camp. She quickly woke her family and hustled them out. Before leaving, she wrapped a buffalo skin around the pet crane and told him to walk in circles around the fire casting the reflection of a child. She hoped to fool her enemies to buy time for her family to escape. Her enemies were indeed fooled and the family escaped. The next day they returned to find their home torn apart and their poor pet crane dead. Not only had he saved them from starving, but also he gave his life to save theirs.

THE FROGS AND THE CRANE:
A SIOUX TALE

A peaceful pond in the middle of the trees was the happy home to a large number of frogs. One day, as the frogs sat in their pond boasting to each other about which was the most important, Crane slowly made his way through the reeds. Just as Crane was about to stab at the loudest boasting frog, he felt something encircle his leg. It was a water snake – mmm, also a nice dinner. This time the boastful frog was spared due to the distraction of the snake.

After a while, Crane became hungry again and went after a second boastful frog, who was too busy bragging to see the danger. But once again, just as the crane was about to strike – he saw a mink out of the corner of his eye. Crane quickly flew away. The second arrogant frog had been spared without even knowing it. Later, Crane returned and tried for another frog, who was boasting the loudest that he was king of the pond. Just as Crane had him by the leg, a fox came up from behind and carried Crane off. A third frog had now escaped Crane's beak, but he was badly injured and never spoke again. The lesson of the story is that it is unwise to boast too loudly.

THE RACE BETWEEN THE CRANE AND THE HUMMINGBIRD

This tale is frequently attributed to the Cherokee, although versions appear in the lore of many southeastern Native Americans.

The Crane and the Hummingbird were both in love with the same beautiful maiden. She much preferred the Hummingbird to the Crane. She thought the Hummingbird very handsome and agile, and the Crane quite gangly and awkward. The Crane, however, was very persistent in his attentions toward her. In order to get rid of the pesky Crane, the young maiden said she would marry the winner of a race between the two. Now, the maiden believed the Hummingbird to be the fleeter of the two, and was not particularly worried that she would have to marry the big Crane. She did not know the Crane could fly all night.

The birds agreed to fly the circumference of the world. The fastest one would marry her when he returned. The Hummingbird shot off lickety split with the Crane flapping heavily behind. When Hummingbird stopped to rest at nightfall he was confident that he was far ahead of Crane. Little did he know that Crane soon passed him because he flew steadily all night long. Hummingbird began again in the morning and was surprised to see Crane stopped by a creek eating crayfish for breakfast. Puzzled, he flew past Crane still confident he would easily win the race. The day proceeded as before. When Hummingbird stopped to sleep, Crane easily passed him during the night. Hummingbird caught up to Crane the following day, but each day Crane gained more and more distance, until on the seventh day Crane was an entire day ahead of Hummingbird. On the morning of the seventh day Crane arrived at the beautiful maiden's house.

Hummingbird did not arrive until that evening. The beautiful maiden was so upset by the outcome of the race that she decided to remain unmarried for the rest of her life.

THE QUALITY OF CRANE

WHY CRANE STANDS IN WATER

This Cherokee myth is about the time before there were people, and the animals were in charge of the fire.

Before there were people on earth, the animals held dances every month to help the seasons change. In those days, Cranes still had feathers on their legs.

At one dance, Crane, who was known as the most graceful dancer, was showing off for the other animals, and danced a bit too close to the fire. To his horror, his beautiful leg feathers caught on fire.

Shocked, Crane ran screaming to the river and jumped in. Steam rose from the water. Crane slowly picked up his smoldering legs only to see that all the beautiful feathers had been scorched off his legs.

All the animals at the dance told Crane the danger was over and asked Crane to come out of the water and dance some more. Poor Crane, however, was too embarrassed by his bare and ugly legs, and wouldn't come out of the water. The animals concluded that Crane was punished for his arrogance and self-serving dancing. He should have been dancing to help the seasons, not to show off his beauty.

To this day, Crane wades in the water ashamed to show his bare legs.

CRANE BRIDGE

The long legs and beak of the crane are the inspiration for a bridge motif in some Native American folk tales. Legends tell of Grandfather Crane offering his long legs to fugitives as a bridge so they can flee across rivers in their path. However, when their pursuers attempt to cross, Grandfather Crane withdraws his leg-bridge causing them to fall into the water. In some variations of the story, it is the long neck of Grandfather Crane that is employed as a bridge.

Once, long ago, Bear Woman was chasing some children and threatening to eat them. The children ran away as fast as they could, but Bear Woman was gaining steadily on them. The children burst out of the forest and came upon a river bank where they saw Grandfather Crane wading in the cool water. "Oh, please Grandfather Crane, stretch your long legs across the river to help us escape Bear Woman – or she will eat us!" Grandfather Crane was happy to oblige the children and stretched his long legs across the water. The children quickly scrambled across this avian bridge to the other side.

Before Grandfather Crane could retract his long legs, Bear Woman began to dash across the makeshift bridge. Just as she was over the middle of the water, Grandfather crane pulled back his legs and Bear Woman fell into the river and floated away.

A Shoshoni version of this story has a Coyote chasing Rabbit. When Rabbit reaches the river he pleads with Uncle Crane to help him cross. Uncle Crane obliges and Rabbit makes it to safety. When Coyote attempts to cross the river – Uncle Crane dumps him in the river.

CRY OF THE CRANE

The Miami, a tribe of North American Indians of Algonquian origin were named for the call of the crane. The English called them Twightwee, a corruption of the native name, which literally meant the cry of the crane. They were first found in southeastern Wisconsin, and in 1764 numbered about 1,750. Their civilization was advanced and they lived in stockaded towns. They took part in Pontiac's conspiracy in 1764 and in the American War of Independence. During the War of 1812 they fought on the English side. By the close of this war they were greatly reduced in numbers.

CRANES IN ASIA

Why do cranes figure so prominently in Asian art? They are a favorite subject for paintings, silk screens, origami, ceramics, and of course folklore. They adorn the walls of restaurants, greeting cards, chopsticks, and lampshades. The answer lies in the symbolic value of the cranes, and their proximity to human populations in many parts of Asia. Next to the phoenix, which is an imaginary bird, the crane is perhaps the most celebrated bird in Chinese legends.

Nine of the fifteen species of cranes occur in various parts of Asia, although it is interesting that in early Chinese texts, species are not differentiated. The name *he* applies to all species of cranes. The differences in color and appearance are attributed to age and longevity of the bird – the older they are, the darker their feathers become. "In a thousand years, cranes alter to gray; in another thousand years they alter to black" (Schafer, 1983). A black crane was considered to be such an auspicious omen, that it must be reported immediately to the emperor.

Cranes of Asia: Red-crowned Crane, Hooded Crane, White-naped Crane, Eurasian Crane, Siberian Crane, Black-necked Crane, Demoiselle Crane, Sarus Crane, and Sandhill Cranes nest in Siberia.

SYMBOLS OF LONG LIFE AND IMMORTALITY

The crane in Asia signifies longevity because they often live to a ripe old age. *He-ling,* "crane age" is a phrase used to describe advancing years. Birthday felicitations in China may include the phrase "may you live as long as a crane."

In Chinese art, cranes are often depicted with other symbols of longevity or immortality, such as tortoises, stones, pine trees, peaches and bamboo. Shou-lao, the ancient Chinese Taoist god of long life and luck, is usually portrayed with an enormous head and carrying a long staff with a gourd that contains the water of life. In his other hand he holds the peach of immortality often with a crane perched on top.

LONGEVITY RECORD

It is perhaps with good reason that cranes are a symbol of longevity. The longest living crane in recorded history is Wolf, a Siberian Crane *Grus leucogeranus*, who lived at the International Crane Foundation in Baraboo, Wisconsin. Wolf was born at a zoo in Switzerland in 1905 and died in Baraboo at the ripe old age of 82. He fathered a chick when he was in his 70s. Even at 82 Wolf did not die of old age. He died of an accidental head trauma, so it's possible he could have lived even longer. Wolf's longevity record is listed in the *Guinness Book of World Records.*

RECIPE FOR LONGEVITY AND IMMORTALITY

An early Chinese written reference to the use of cranes in a medicinal way is found in the *Han Shu* (also known as The Book of Han, a classic Chinese history of the Western Han Dynasty) dating to the Wang Mang period A.D. 9-24, where crane is mentioned in the *Jiaosizhi* as an ingredient in a recipe for longevity. The relevant passage reads as follows:

> "Cook the brain of a crane with the shell of a large tortoise and also the rhinoceros jade [horn]. Then take the juice and soak seeds in them. Then plant the seeds and eat the grain which grows from them and you will become immortal".

CRANE BRAIN

The *Materia Medica*, a Ming Dynasty (1368-1644) pharmacology compilation, describes the medicinal purposes of cranes. Ingested crane brain was thought to improve eyesight and the ability to see in the dark. Crane's blood might increase vitality and energy, as well as help the lungs. Crane eggs were thought to lessen the severity of smallpox. It was also believed that the substance making up the red crown of the crane was poisonous and could be used as a weapon against enemies or to commit suicide. Today, however, cranes are protected in China.

IMMORTALS AND CRANES

A being that has attained physical immortality in religious Taoism is called Xian. A Xian is no longer subject to the *world of dust* and is a master in various magical skills. These immortals are often portrayed riding cranes. Over the centuries various famous and venerated historical personalities were admitted to the ranks of the immortals. The best known is the Ba Xian (the eight immortals). Amulets and charms bearing the symbols of the Xian are believed to bring good fortune, thus the popularity of cranes on jewelry, fans and combs.

LAN CAI-HE

One peculiar tale of the Chinese Ba Xian is that of Lan Cai-he. He dresses in rags, wears a belt made of black wood, and wears a boot on one foot while the other foot is bare. In summer he wears a thick overcoat but dresses lightly in winter. His breath is like hot steam. According to legend he roamed the streets as a beggar, accompanying his songs with castanets, and is inebriated most of the time. When people give him money, he strings the coins on a cord, which he drags behind him. One day he entered an inn, stripped off his clothes, and disappeared into the clouds riding on a crane, a not uncommon motif in Asian folklore – riding on a crane.

JUROJIN

As in Chinese folklore, the Japanese also consider the crane (tsuru) a symbol of long life. Jurojin, the Japanese Shinto god of longevity and happy old age, is one of the Shichi Fukujin, the seven gods of luck. A crane and a tortoise accompany Jurojin. He is often painted riding a white stag, a happy and friendly old man.

(tsuru)

ON THE WINGS OF CRANES

Cranes represent not only respected Asian ideals, but they are also depicted as adventurous figures in many legends – particularly as a heavenly mode of transportation. Immortals ride on the backs of cranes. They often disappear from earth on cranes. Another motif is that of turning into a crane or re-visiting earth in the form of a crane.

Japanese creation myths tell of a great ancient warrior who conquered many enemies in order to create and expand his kingdom of Japan. It was said that when the great man died, he took the form of a crane and flew into the heavens.

The crane riders are usually portrayed in or near clouds, which gives them the appearance of being very lofty. Both Korean and Vietnamese folklore maintain that the souls of departed loved ones are transported on the wings of cranes to a higher level of consciousness. The custom in one region of China places a crane with out-spread wings on the coffin at a funeral procession, or placing a paper crane in the window of the deceased person likely stems from this belief that the loved one will be conveyed to heaven by a crane.

CRANE AROMATHERAPY

Because of the crane's reputation in Asia as a high flier and a means of transportation to lofty places, in ancient times cranes warranted their very own incense.

The incense was used to attract the cranes back into the secular world. The literal translation of the incense name is *aromatic which brings down the realized ones.* From the writings of a T'ang (A.D. 626-755) poet it is known that the incense was made from the scented heartwood of a rosewood liana. It is not uncommon to see incense burners featuring flying cranes.

CRANE CABARET

Early Chinese texts reveal that wealthy Chinese not only kept cranes as valued pets, but also trained them to perform. The cranes' spectacular dance was a favorite entertainment. Writings indicate that cranes were considered very intelligent birds and highly trainable performers. A very early description of cranes is contained in the history book *Zuo Zhuan* (4th century B.C.).

The *Zuo Zhuan* also relates the story of Duke Yi from the state of Wei, who loved cranes. Duke Yi's cranes maintained a very high status in his household, and were said to even travel in carriages. The soldiers of Duke Yi begrudged the cranes this attention. They felt the cranes were treated better than they were.

Another important man who kept cranes was Grand General Yan Hu (Western Jin Dynasty 221-278). He was garrisoned in Hubei Province where cranes were numerous in the wild. He captured many of the cranes and taught them to dance to amuse his guests.

GAOQIAO: WALKING ON STILTS

In China, "Gaoqiao" performers tie two long stilts to their feet. Great skill and practice is required to perform Gaoqiao. Scholars believe the Gaoqiao originated from the totem worship of primitive clans and the fishermen who lived along the coast. Historians say that the Danzhu clan in the times of Yao and Shun emperors, who had the crane as their totem, walked on stilts to imitate the movements of the crane.

CRANE CONTEMPLATION

Early Chinese poets refer to cranes kept in captivity, and also when writing about romance and devotion. Later, the crane in Chinese literature is more closely associated with scholarly hermits or people who study astronomy. This is probably due to the crane's conspicuous stance, which was thought to epitomize contemplation and deep thought.

BADGES OF PRESTIGE

During the Manchu Ching dynasty (1644-1912), government officials flaunted elaborate embroidered badges, which portrayed their rank and importance in China's civil service. There were nine ranks and a bird, such as peacock, oriole, egret, or duck, represented each rank. The symbol for the highest civil rank was the revered crane.

THE CRANE ON THE WALL:
A JAPANESE TALE

Once, long ago, an old man came into a wine shop to buy sake. He said, "I have no money, but I would like to have some sake." The shopkeeper looked at the ragged old man and said, "You may have the sake for free." There was an odd quality about the old man that made the shopkeeper feel generous.

The old man enjoyed the sake there in the store and then left. He came back to the shop the next day, and the events of the day before were repeated. The same happened for quite a few days until one day the old man said, "I have been drinking your sake and I will now re-pay you for your kindness with a drawing." The old man drew a crane on the wall of the wine shop. He said, "Tell your customers to look at the crane, clap their hands, and sing."

When the next customer came in and did as he was told, the crane magically came to life and began dancing in the wine shop. Everyone in the shop was delighted with the beautiful dancing crane. Soon, the dancing crane was the talk of the town, and the shopkeeper was thrilled with a tremendous increase in his business.

Many years passed, but eventually the old man returned to his drawing of the crane. He pulled out a flute and began playing it. The crane immediately came to life and stepped out of the drawing. The old man climbed onto the crane's back and they flew out and up into the clouds.

TALE OF THE TSURU

Tsuru is the Japanese word for crane.

Once upon a time, a mighty warrior was out hunting with his falcon. The skilled falcon brought down a large crane, which fell at the warrior's feet. The tsuru boldly looked into the great warrior's eyes, unafraid. He was prepared to die with honor.

The warrior felt a surge of admiration for the bird's courage and spirit. He released the bird and vowed to never hunt again. He retired to a monastery where he lived to be a "crane's age" and became a famous poet. It is said that from that time on, the tsuru became the symbol of long life, courage and good fortune in Japan.

EARLY BIRD BANDING?

Today it is not uncommon for scientists to place leg bands on birds to monitor their numbers and movements. Perhaps modern day scientists would be surprised to know of an old Buddhist practice from 11th and 12th century Japan. That is, the practice of attaching prayer strips to the legs of birds and then releasing them to honor men lost in battle.

Indeed, this Buddhist practice may have inspired Yorimoto (1147-1199), a powerful Japanese shogun in the 12th century, to attach labels to the legs of cranes and then release them. He asked that people who subsequently captured the birds record their location on the label and let them go. Legend spread that several of Yorimoto's cranes were still alive centuries later, reinforcing the notion of the cranes' amazing longevity.

HERALDRY

The themes of vigilance and longevity are manifested in the use of cranes in heraldry. Heraldry is an ancient form of identification often used to recognize families or clans using emblems. Cranes were frequently carved on family crests in medieval Japan.

THE CRANE AND THE TURTLE:
A JAPANESE TALE

Long ago, a turtle lived in a small pond that was drying up because there was no rain. The turtle asked a passing crane what he should do. "You should move to a larger pond, this one is shrinking," said the crane, who knew a lot about water and ponds. "But Tsuru-san where is such a pond and how would I get there?" The crane answered, "I visit many ponds, and I know there is a nice big pond on the other side of this mountain and there are lots of turtles there floating, eating and having a marvelous time. You should go there."

The turtle liked the idea of floating in a spacious pond and having a good time with other turtles, but then he realized he would have to walk over a mountain to reach it. He knew he would never make it. The crane came to his rescue and offered to fly him there. The crane used his loud trumpeting call to summon another crane to help with the turtle. The two cranes grasped with their beaks a long stick on either end and told the turtle to grab hold of the stick in the middle with his strong teeth and jaw, and they would fly him over the mountain between them. "Oh thank you, Tsuru-san!" exclaimed the turtle.

And so the journey began, they flew and flew. The cranes flew over a village and the turtle looked down to see children pointing at him and staring. The children had never seen such a sight and laughed wildly. This angered the proud little turtle. He yelled at the children to be quiet and not be so rude, but as soon as he opened his mouth to speak, he realized his mistake. But it was too late for the little turtle. He hurtled downward and fell to the ground below landing on his back. Luckily he had a hard shell to protect him, but to this day, the pattern of cracks in the turtle's shell is still visible.

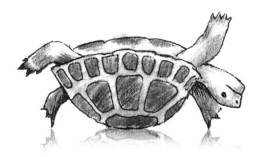

ENCHANTED BRIDE

In many cultures there are folktales based on the theme of a bird turning into a woman. In European tales the bird is often portrayed as a swan. In Asia, the bird is usually a crane. There are over two hundred recorded variations of this motif, that is, a crane as an enchanted bride. The person rescuing the crane in the story is usually a farmer, fisherman, woodcutter, or even a poor childless couple.

Read more about it:

Bartoli, Jennifer, and Kozo Shimizu. *The Story of the Grateful Crane a Japanese Folktale.* Chicago: A. Whitman, 1977.

Bodkin, Odds, and Gennadii Spirin. *The Crane Wife.* San Diego: Harcourt Brace, 1998.

Kakkenbusshu, Hiroko, Yasuji Mori, and Kazue Ito. *Tsuru No Ongaeshi/The Grateful Crane.* Kodansha Nihongo Folktales Series 3. Tokyo, New York: Kodansha International, 1993.

Keo, Ena. *The Crane Wife* [Tsuru Nyobo]. Austin, TX: Steck-Vaughnco. 1998.

Kuwata, Masakazu. *The Grateful Crane.* Tokyo: Kodansha International, 1963.

Matsutani, Miyoko. *The Crane Maiden* [Tsuru No Ongaeshi]. New York: Parents' Magazine Press, 1968.

Seki, Keigo. *Folktales of Japan.* Chicago: University of Chicago Press, 1963.

Yagawa, Sumiko, and Suekichi Akaba. *The Crane Wife.* New York: William Morrow, 1981.

THE SWORD:
A JAPANESE TALE

A nobleman who was down on his luck went to live in the countryside. While out walking one day he saw a hunter about to kill a crane he had captured. The nobleman pleaded for the life of the crane. The hunter spared the crane's life in exchange for the nobleman's sword, his only remaining prized possession. The next day a beautiful girl came to the nobleman's door asking for shelter. He granted her wish and they eventually became a couple and married.

Years later, the local landowner decided to have a big hunting party. The beautiful girl heard of it, and confessed to her husband that she was the crane he saved that day long ago, and that she must now flee and return to the kingdom of the birds. He decided to go with her and they fled to the home of her parents.

TSURU NO ONGAESHI: *The Grateful Crane*
TSURU NYOBO: *The Crane Wife*

Once upon a time, there was a poor hunter. One day, he came upon a trapped crane. He took pity on the crane and released it. A few days later, a lovely woman visited his house, and asked him for shelter. Eventually the two were married. As well as being beautiful, the bride had a nice disposition. They were happy, except that they were very poor. One day, the wife said she would weave cloth so that he could sell it to make money. But she told him that he was never to see her weaving. After three days in a weaving hut she came out with a beautiful fabric. The hunter took the fabric to town, where the merchants were surprised and paid gold for it. The fabric was a very rare one called Tsuru-no-senba-ori (thousand feathers of crane).

After that, the wife wove the valuable fabric several times. They lived in comfort and prosperity. The hunter grew accustomed to the new lifestyle and urged her to keep weaving. Gradually, however, his wife grew weak and thin. Finally, she said that she could no longer weave the beautiful cloth. Her greedy husband asked her to weave just once more. At last she was persuaded to do so and started to weave again. That time, she didn't come out on the third day. Three more days passed. The husband became worried, and finally broke his promise, peering in at her weaving. To his surprise, it was not a woman but a crane that was weaving. On the next morning, his wife came out with the last fabric in her hands. She said "You have seen my true form, so I cannot stay here." She transformed herself back into a crane and flew away.

SENBAZURU: *Thousand Cranes*

In Japan, the thousand-crane motif *senbazuru* (zuru (tsuru) = crane) likely originated with the 17th century artist Sotatsu. Sotatsu painted a very famous scroll. The 50-foot-long scroll featured classical poems, as well as many, many cranes beautifully painted and exhibiting diverse behaviors. The thousand-crane theme caught on with other artists such as woodblock printers, ceramic artists, and silk painters and was henceforth popular with the masses. The Red-crowned Crane is the favorite subject, but occasionally other crane species are portrayed. Often the artists had never actually seen a crane, so it is not uncommon to see anatomically incorrect cranes.

ORIGAMI CRANES

In the late 18th century a book was published in Kyoto detailing how to fold a thousand paper cranes. Cranes were said to live for a thousand years. Folded cranes were and still are a popular gift on birthdays. A garland of origami cranes might also be given to someone who is ill.

SADAKO

Probably the most famous story about folded cranes is that of Sadako and the thousand paper cranes. It is the story of a girl who survived the bombing of Hiroshima, Japan only to later develop leukemia from exposure to radiation. Japanese legend maintains that anyone who folds 1,000 origami cranes will receive one wish. Sadako works diligently to fold cranes in order to receive her wish of a full recovery. Sadako did not live long enough to fold a thousand cranes, but her efforts and story became an international symbol for peace.

At the Peace Park in Hiroshima is a large statue to honor Sadako. It shows a young girl holding a folded crane. These lines are inscribed on the monument:

I will write peace on your wings

And you will fly all over the world

Children all over the world have joined the Thousand Cranes Peace Network and folded paper cranes that are placed at the base of the Children's Monument.

CRANES IN HAIKU

There is a Red-crowned Crane at the International Crane Foundation named Haiku in honor of this concise form of poetry. Haiku poetry came into existence during the Edo period (1603-1867) of Japanese history.

> *The world?*
> *Moonlit drops shaken*
> *From the crane's bill.*
> — Dogen, 1200-1253

The poet still considered the most accomplished and masterful was Matsuo Basho (1644-1694). Basho traveled extensively throughout his lifetime observing the nuances of life and nature, and then pouring them into his poetry. Basho wrote several haiku about cranes, translated here:

> *Cool seascape with cranes*
> *Wading long-legged in the pools*
> *Mid the Tideway dunes.*

> *Patiently fishing in the lake*
> *the crane's long legs have shortened*
> *since the rains.*

> *The shallows –*
> *a crane's thighs splashed*
> *in cool waves.*

PLAYING FAVORITES

Although there are six species of cranes in East Asia, the historic record clearly shows that the Red-crowned Crane *Grus japonensis* is the favorite of the Chinese, Japanese, and Koreans. This crane is also known in English as the Manchurian crane or the Japanese crane. It is a common theme in popular culture and the decorative arts. In South Korea, the Red-crowned Crane is so beloved that it was named National Natural Treasure no. 202.

AS LONG AS WE BOTH SHALL LIVE...

In Japan the Red-crowned Crane is called *tancho,* which means red crown. Their regal beauty and unique unison call have captivated Asian artists throughout the ages. Red-crowned Cranes are often portrayed on wedding kimonos because they are thought to be monogamous and pair for life. Indeed cranes are devoted couples and extraordinarily grief-stricken and inconsolable when one loses a partner. In ancient times, it was thought that they would never "re-marry" and would live out their lives as melancholy wanderers. Today scientists know that cranes likely do re-pair if a compatible mate can be found, but that doesn't minimize their widespread reputation as a steadfast partner.

CRANE KIMONO

A wedding kimono portraying cranes is symbolic of marital fidelity. The white feathers of the crane symbolize the purity of the bride and the bright red head, the vitality of the groom. The red and white color scheme of cranes is still a very popular color combination in Asia, as are items portraying cranes during the engagement and wedding festivities. A gift of money to the new couple might be conveyed inside a special crane festooned envelope, or a wedding cake may be adorned with cranes.

SCULPTURE

In Beijing, China, two crane sculptures vigilantly stand guard in the Forbidden City. They are probably the most famous crane sculptures in the world.

The Red-crowned Crane is the subject of another magnificent sculpture in Washington, D.C. at the National Japanese American Memorial. The sculpture is 14 feet high and depicts two bronze cranes entwined and trapped in barbed wire. The birds grasp the wire in their beaks in a valiant effort to break free. The cranes symbolize the Japanese American experience during World War II.

SYMBOLS OF PARENTAL VIGILANCE

Cranes in the wild are excellent and vigilant parents. They share equally between male and female the difficult task of rearing chicks in a harsh world. This devotion is particularly admired in Chinese culture.

Five birds represent the five relationships between people: the phoenix, Mandarin duck, heron, wagtail and the crane. The crane symbolizes the father/son relationship.

AINU LEGENDS

The indigenous people native to Hokkaido, Japan are known as the Ainu. The Ainu practice Animism, the belief that everything in nature has a spirit or god on the inside. The Red-crowned Crane is beloved by the Ainu. They are known as *sarorun chikap,* or bird among the tall grasses and also *sarorun kamui,* or marsh god. The Ainu believe the inner lining of the crane's nest is made of a special material called *setsambe,* which means, "the heart of the nest." If a person discovers setsambe, it is considered a great treasure that will bring prosperity. Women particularly appreciate setsambe and keep it as a charm. They believe it will bring a good harvest and skill in their needlework.

The Ainu find the Red-crowned Crane so beautiful, they believe they are dressed in clothing from heaven. The Ainu women perform a crane dance where they hold their shawls around themselves to look like the wings of a crane and copy the calls of the crane as they dance. Another crane dance is called Tokachi where two young girls dance around a third who portrays the chick.

NATIONAL BIRDS IN AFRICA

Six of the fifteen species of cranes live in Africa. The Black Crowned Crane *Balearica pavonina*, national bird of Nigeria, is resident in the Sahel region of western and central Africa. The Grey Crowned Crane *Balearica regulorum*, national bird of Uganda, spans eastern and southern Africa. The Wattled Crane *Bugeranus carunculatus*, largest and rarest of Africa's cranes, ranges from Ethiopia to South Africa. The Blue Crane *Anthropoides paradisea*, national bird of South Africa, is endemic to the grasslands of South Africa and Namibia. The Demoiselle Crane *Anthropoides virgo* is a winter visitor to northeastern Africa, with possibly a small resident population in the Atlas Mountains of Morocco. The Eurasian Crane *Grus grus* is a winter visitor to northern Africa.

(flag of Uganda)

CROWNS FOR CRANES

The spectacular crowned cranes of Africa garner the most attention in African legends. A well-known story explains how the cranes obtained their golden crowns. Biologists hypothesize that the beautiful crowns evolved as sun shades against the hot African sun, or as camouflage in the vast grasslands — but a much different explanation for their yellow headdress is described in "How the Cranes Got their Crowns." This story originates near Lake Victoria (Nyansa).

> A great king was stranded on the vast plains on a very hot day. He was feeling faint from the heat, and wanted to rest in the shade. He entreated various birds and animals for help during his wanderings, but none would help him. He was becoming weak and very angry, until he met a flock of cranes. The king asked the cranes for help and they gladly shaded the old king with their beautiful wings and helped him to some shady trees. The king quickly recovered his strength and rejoiced at the kindness and beauty of the cranes.
>
> In thanks, he placed his hand on their heads and there appeared small golden crowns. They were made of real gold! The cranes thanked him for this generous gift and then flew off. The king was pleased with his gift and went home. Several months later, a crane appeared on his doorstep in a bedraggled state – thin, weak, and bleeding. The crane begged the king to take back his gift. He told the king the cranes were now hunted day and night for their golden crown.

The king, realizing his foolishness and the greed and jealousy of others, transformed the gold crowns into a halo of golden feathers, which the cranes still have today.

The moral of the story is that a gift is a great responsibility for the giver, and should not be bestowed without thought as to how the gift will be received.

INDWE

The Zulu people of southern Africa feel a close affinity to the natural world. Birds are prominent in their language and lore. Among the many birds represented in their culture are the greatly revered Blue Cranes *Anthropoides paradisea*, or Indwe. The Blue Crane is the only crane species with no trace of red on its head. Instead, to ward off predators, it puffs up its smooth grey-blue head like a cobra, and hisses, dancing aggressively toward its predators. The Zulu people often look for Blue Cranes as they walk through the veld to find their cattle. Veld is an Afrikaans word meaning open grassland, and in southern Africa they are typically used for grazing livestock. If one sees a crane, cattle may be nearby because the cranes and cattle have a symbiotic relationship. The cranes eat the insects and seeds that are disturbed as the cattle graze.

The use of bird feathers for decorative purposes is a common practice. Only the royal family, however, may use feathers of the Blue Crane in their headdress. The Blue Crane is a symbol for the Zulu Royal House. King Shaka Zulu (c. 1781-1828) was known to use the long black wing feathers of the Blue Crane in his regal headdress because he believed it would give him extraordinary powers to predict the weather.

XHOSA

Cranes of southern Africa are revered by the Xhosa people. The Xhosa are an ethnic group of Bantu origin, living mainly in the Eastern Cape Province. Traditionally, the Xhosa were farmers and cattle herders. Their Bantu language belongs to the Niger-Congo family and is similar to Zulu.

The Xhosa people believe that if a crowned crane is killed, death will afflict the hunter's family. Brave warriors wore Blue Crane, or Indwe, feathers during battle. The feathers were presented at a special ceremony by the chief to honor a feat of bravery and were worn on the head. The use of Blue Crane feathers was only permitted for battle.

CRANE TEACHES JACKAL TO FLY:
A KHOIKHOI FOLKTALE

The Khoikhoi are a nomadic pastoral people of southwestern Africa (Namibia, and western South Africa). They historically inhabited the coast of the Cape of Good Hope, but were displaced by European settlers. They herded cattle on vast grasslands. Blue Cranes, the national bird of South Africa, also inhabited these grasslands.

High up in a plum tree lived a mother dove and her two offspring. One day a jackal came around the tree attracted by the lullaby the mother dove was singing to her chicks. The jackal was very hungry and demanded one of the chicks as a meal or he threatened to climb up and eat both chicks. The terrified dove forgot that jackals can't climb trees, so she threw one chick down to save the other. The jackal devoured the chick and demanded the other. If she did not comply, he threatened to climb up and eat her too. Alas, the distraught dove threw down her second chick to save herself. Satisfied, the jackal ran away.

The grieving dove told her story to her neighbor the Blue Crane. The Blue Crane reminded the dove that jackals can't climb trees and that her chicks were safe high in the tree. The dove realized how badly she had been tricked by the jackal. The Blue Crane decided to play a trick on the jackal, leading him to believe that he could learn to fly. The jackal was very tired from running around all the time and agreed that flying would be much easier. He promised to do whatever the crane said in order to learn to fly. First, she told the jackal to smear himself with sticky gum from the gum tree. The jackal complied. The crane then plucked some of

THE QUALITY OF CRANES

her own feathers and applied them to the sticky jackal. The jackal was impressed with his new plumage although it was a bit uncomfortable.

The crane told the jackal to climb onto her back and she would fly high into the sky. "When I tell you to jump off and fly, you must do it," said the crane. The jackal jumped off the crane when they were high above the earth, but he forgot to flap his wings, and instead let out a loud bellow. He landed on the ground with such force that the two baby doves he had eaten earlier in the day, burst out of his mouth. The crane carried the little doves back to their mother. The jackal crept to the river to clean himself and all the other animals laughed at his ridiculous appearance. The crane wisely said, "He who tricks others, will then be tricked himself."

AUSTRALIA

The two crane species occurring in Australia are the Brolga *Grus rubicunda,* also known in Australia as the "native companion," and the Australian Sarus Crane *Grus antigone gilli.* The word Brolga derives from the Gamilaraay (also spelled Kamilaroi) word **burralga.** Gamilaraay is an Australian Aboriginal language that was once spoken over a vast area of north-central New South Wales. The Brolga is a large bird and interestingly the word in Gamilaraay for "big" is burrul.

Brolgas have developed physiological and behavioral adaptations to Australia's diverse and extreme climatic conditions. They are the only crane with a salt gland located near the eye, which allows them to excrete a concentrated salt solution from the brackish water they sometimes drink.

BROLGA, THE DANCING GIRL

Legend has it that the Brolga *Grus rubicunda* was named for a beautiful maiden.

Brolga was the most popular girl in her village. She was beautiful, but more importantly, she was an excellent dancer. Brolga was not satisfied to beat the drums with the other women for the men dancers. She danced with the men and even created new dances. She became very famous for her dancing skill, and people came from all over to watch her. Many men desired her hand in marriage, but Brolga always refused. Dancing was her only love.

Nonega, an evil magician, also wanted to marry Brolga. She refused him too. In anger, he proclaimed that no one would have her if he couldn't. The next day when Brolga was dancing alone, a strange whirlwind approached her. Nonega was in the center of the swirling cloud chanting magical spells. The whirlwind engulfed Brolga and left in her place a tall graceful bird. The bird was dancing just where Brolga had been. When the people saw the bird dancing they cried out "Brolga! Brolga!" The bird nodded and bowed and from thenceforth the statuesque bird was called Brolga.

THE CREATION OF FIRE

Australian aboriginal people are thought to have the oldest continuously maintained cultural history on earth, possibly more than 50,000 years old. In Australian aboriginal lore, the Dreamtime is the mystical past when spirit gods inhabited the earth. The following story takes place during the days just after the Dreamtime. The motif is similar to a variety of native North American stories connecting Crane with fire or as the "keeper of fire."

> Long ago, the people did not know how to make fire, and so could not cook their food. At that time the Crane, *Booroolgah* was married to the Kangaroo Rat, *Goonur.* One day Crane was messing around with two sticks, rubbing them together. Suddenly smoke rose from the sticks and Kangaroo Rat, seeing the opportunity, ran for dry leaves and sticks to bolster the spark. To their amazement, the spark grew to a flame and Crane and Kangaroo Rat were thrilled to realize they had created fire and could now cook their food. Everyone knows that cooked food tastes better than raw food.

> Crane and Kangaroo Rat did not share their discovery and took great pains to keep the creation of fire a secret. They always carried a firestick in a pouch with them and were careful that no one from their tribe saw them light a fire or cook their fish. Despite their efforts, the delicious aroma of the cooking food aroused suspicion, and Owl and Parrot were sent to spy on them. Owl and Parrot saw them blow on their firestick and create a great roaring fire to cook food.

The tribe decided to set a trap. They would hold a corroboree (a dance ceremony) and invite Crane and Kangaroo Rat. They hoped that the excitement of the dancing would make the pair forget about their treasure pouch. It would be Hawk's job to steal the pouch when it was unattended. Indeed, during the dancing of the special dance named for the crane, *The Brolga,* Hawk was able to steal the pouch and fly away dropping fire everywhere on the landscape. Crane and Kangaroo Rat pursued, but soon realized the futility of trying to stop Hawk, so they resigned themselves to share the fire with everyone. The events were the origin of fire and cooked food.

HOW THE SUN WAS MADE

During the Dreamtime, before there were even people on the earth, there was no light because there was no sun. The world was in darkness except for some faint light from the stars and moon.

One dark day, Emu or Dinewan, and Crane Brolga, were having a big fight, although no one really remembers why. At one point, Crane became so angry with Emu, she snatched a fresh egg from Emu's nest. She threw it as hard as she could up into the gloomy sky. On the way up, it hit the branch of a tree and broke open. The golden yolk tumbled out and dripped down toward earth. The yellow yolk fell upon a pile of dry branches which instantly caught fire. The fire sent up a beautiful glow upon the dark and shadowy earth. A spirit in the heavens looked down upon this attractive sight and thought the earth looked so charming bathed in this soft glow.

The spirit decided to make a fire each and every day for the earth and its inhabitants. Helper spirits collected firewood all during the night and made great piles. Just before they were ready to light the piles, they sent out the morning star as a warning that the fire would soon be lit. Many of the earth's inhabitants, however, slept through this announcement, so the spirits thought there should be noise added to wake them. The spirits then sent the Kookaburra to laugh loudly as the new day was dawning. Parents, who remembered the days of darkness, forbade their children to laugh at the silly Kookaburra lest they insult him and cause the darkness to return.

EMU AND BROLGA

A Kamilaroi story from Australia explains why Crane only lays two eggs and why Emu doesn't fly. There are several recorded variations of this story.

In the old, old days Emu and Brolga both had many children. Emu and Brolga often went together to forage for food. One day Emu decided to play a trick on Brolga, and came to the foraging place with only two of her children. Brolga asked Emu, "Where are your children?" Emu replied, "I killed them because it is too difficult to feed them all. You should ask your husband if you might kill yours. Life will be easier for you." "Yes, I will ask my husband if I may kill my children," said Brolga.

The next day at the foraging place, Brolga only had two children with her. When Emu saw that her trick worked and that Brolga had killed her other children, she smugly brought out all of her own children, who were hidden away. They were not dead. Brolga was very sad at being tricked into killing her children and she went away. When she returned she began foraging with Emu with her wings tucked up and hidden behind her back. Puzzled, Emu said, "Why do you eat like that?" "Oh, I cut off my wings because it is a much better way to eat and look for food. You should ask your husband if you may cut off your wings." The next day, Emu appeared with no wings, and Brolga triumphantly danced and spread her own wings. She flew into the sky calling to Emu, "You are forever destined to stay on the ground, while I dance and fly with my beautiful wings."

This is why Brolga dances to this day and lays only two eggs and why Emu doesn't fly at all.

CRANE'S LONG BEAK

An aboriginal folktale from the Gumatj clan of Australia explains how the crane got his long beak and flies with his legs outstretched behind him:

> Once, long ago Emu was busy carving a beautiful, long spear. Not far away, Crane was cooking a dinner. Everyone knew it was not a good idea to be carving a spear so near someone cooking. So, Emu said, "Go away Crane. Cook somewhere else. My work is important."
>
> Of course this angered Crane, who thought his work was important too. Crane stirred up his fire, threw burning coals at Emu, and then flew away. Emu quickly brushed off the smoldering embers and took aim with his spear at Crane. But Crane was swift, and was already flying out of reach of the spear.
>
> Now Emu was really angry. He placed his spear in a spear thrower and again took aim at Crane. But Crane was now in the clouds where Emu could not see him.
>
> Emu did not give up though, and waited patiently. When Crane flew out of the clouds, Emu took aim carefully and threw his spear. It hit Crane from behind and came out the front through his mouth.
>
> Crane fell out of the sky. He tried to pull the spear out, but it was lodged so tightly, he was unable to pull it free. At last Crane gave up on the spear and decided to leave it where it was. "I'll leave this spear and let my children use it after me."

And that is why today Crane has a long beak and flies with his legs stretched out behind him.

SNOW WREATH

In Russia, the Siberian Crane *Grus leucogeranus,* is called the "snow wreath" because the bird is almost completely white. The indigenous people of Siberia have traditionally protected this crane because they believe it is a symbol for luck and good health. The birds were always left undisturbed in their marshy breeding grounds because the Khanty people of western Siberia thought that disturbing the crane families would bring bad luck. The Siberian Crane is listed by the International Union for the Conservation of Nature (IUCN) as a critically endangered species, with hunting being one of the threats to its continued existence. Although hunted along its flyway, the Snow Wreath arrives in Siberia for nesting where it benefits from this "mystic" protection bestowed by the Khanty.

CRANE AND HERON:
A RUSSIAN TALE

Once upon a time a Heron and a Crane lived on opposite ends of a big marsh. They each lived all alone and were lonely because of it. One day, Crane went to Heron and said, "Will you marry me, Heron?" Heron replied, "No Crane, I won't be your wife. Your legs are too long, go away."

Crane's feelings were badly hurt by this refusal and he flew back to his end of the marsh. Heron immediately regretted this harsh treatment of Crane and thought it would be nice to have some company and be married. She flew to Crane and said, "I changed my mind Crane. I will marry you."

"Too late," replied Crane. "I don't want to marry you anymore. I don't need a wife. Go away."

After awhile, Crane decided that having a wife was more important than his pride and he flew back to Heron again to plead his case. Again he was refused by Heron, and again Heron soon regretted her decision. This behavior went on and on, back and forth to no avail such that, even today the crane and heron propose to each other, but never marry.

SOUL CRANE!

The crane family is celebrated for its spectacular dancing. Dancing is an important part of the courtship and mating ritual used to synchronize or even stimulate reproduction. It is also thought to strengthen the pair bond between birds.

Crane dancing loosely refers to the actions of bowing, leaping into the air, and flapping the wings. Another component of the dance is picking up dried grass or sticks from the ground with the bill, and tossing them into the air.

Cranes may dance with another crane or even with a larger group.

The cranes were dancing a cotillion as surely as it was danced at Volusia. Two stood apart, erect and white, making a strange music that was part cry and part singing... In the heart of the circle several moved counterclockwise... The dancers raised their wings and lifted their feet, first one and then the other. They sank their heads deep in their snowy breasts, lifted them and sank them again... The outer circle shuffled around and around. The group in the center attained a slow frenzy... Magic birds were dancing in a mystic marsh.

Marjorie Kinnan Rawlings writing about Whooping Cranes in her novel, *The Yearling.*

CRANE DANCING

head bobbing

wing flapping

jumping

bowing

twig tossing

INDIGENOUS CRANE DANCE

Many cultures around the world incorporate animals and birds into ritualistic dancing. Traditional art forms often imitate nature. The crane's conspicuous and delightful dance has captured the attention of many people throughout the ages. Humans have been performing crane dances for thousands of years. People in western Sweden painted pictographs of dancers performing a crane dance over 5,000 years ago and the Khanty of Siberia were known to wear a crane pelt costume and perform a dance after killing a bear in order to drive away the spirit of the dead bear.

In Asia, some traditional exercises, such as in karate and tai chi, copy the graceful movements of cranes. For example, one kata, or position, in karate is called the crane kata. Other cultures known to perform crane dances are: the Ainu of Japan, Koreans, Greeks, as well as indigenous peoples of North America and Australia.

The following passage describes the dancing of the Brolga in Australia:

> *The company dances of the Brolgas are famous.*
> *They were famous before the advent of white men to Australia,*
> *since they formed the basis of spectacular "corroborees"*
> *performed by many tribes of aborigines.*

Chisholm AH. 1948. *Bird Wonders of Australia.* Sydney, Australia: Angus & Robertson.

HAKMU

In Korea, the Hakmu, or Crane Dance dates back at least to the Koryo Dynasty (918-1392) when the crane was revered as one of ten auspicious animals of long life. The Hakmu is a traditional masked folk dance which imitates the graceful movements of the crane such as flying, prancing, bowing and preening. The dance is thought to have originated as a popular folk dance but was later stylized and performed as an official court dance. In 1971, the government designated Hakmu as *Important Intangible Cultural Treasure No. 40*.

THE EXTRAORDINARY STORY OF GEORGE & TEX

Now, to end this little book of crane lore – we come to another story of cranes and humans dancing – but this time they are dancing together. The true story of ornithologist George Archibald and Tex the Whooping Crane is rapidly becoming a legend in its own time.

GEORGE: A man who loved birds since he was a small boy. Co-founder of the International Crane Foundation (ICF).

TEX: A female Whooping Crane imprinted on humans.

> **Imprinting:** Some animals and birds, including cranes, learn their identity during a brief receptive period after birth or hatching. The "imprint" of the individual raising them establishes a long-lasting behavioral response to a specific individual, species or object. A bird strongly imprinted on another species has difficulty accepting a mate of its own species and may never produce offspring.

Tex hatched in 1967 at the San Antonio Zoo. Because previous Whooping Crane chicks at the zoo had all perished, she received special attention from human caretakers to ensure her survival. Unfortunately, she grew up liking humans better than other cranes. As an adult, she would not accept another Whooping Crane as her mate. Sadly, as the years passed, it seemed unlikely that Tex would ever become a mother and help bolster the fading Whooping Crane population. Enter creative thinker Dr. George Archibald! George did not think that Tex was a lost cause. There were so few Whooping Cranes left on earth (only 61 birds in the wild in 1976), that he did not want to squander any opportunity to encourage Tex to lay eggs. He convinced authorities to let him work with Tex and in 1976 brought her to Baraboo,

Wisconsin to the newly formed International Crane Foundation. George believed Tex would lay eggs if she found a suitable mate. He knew she liked human males best – so he had the wild idea to convince her that he could play the role of her "partner." Many people thought George was eccentric and unrealistic to attempt a pair bond with a bird – but George is an optimist in every sense of the word. He persevered.

"I decided to see if she would form a pair bond with me by playing the male role," Archibald said. "This would trigger ovulation, and then artificial insemination might succeed. When she arrived, I put my bed in her house and slept there for a month. I talked to her all the time. As the spring advanced, I began to dance, and she responded. Dancing is how Whooping Cranes initiate mating. It worked. We built a nest together out of corncobs and hay."

— Archibald quoted in the *New Yorker*, May 1982

George isolated himself with Tex and had for company a typewriter, a desk and a cot in a small dwelling affectionately known by the staff as "The Love Shack." George spent countless hours with Tex, which included the celebrated dancing episodes that involved flapping his arms and cavorting about until he was exhausted. Courting Tex occurred in the springtime, and over the years Tex laid several eggs. Even though ICF aviculturists assisted Tex in the reproductive process with artificial insemination, the eggs were either infertile or not viable. Then, in 1982, Tex finally laid the one and only egg that would carry on her important genetic legacy. Under watchful eyes, the egg hatched to become the chick named Gee Whiz. Gee Whiz is still alive at ICF, and has fathered 14 chicks. Many of his descendants have been released into the wild.

The story of George dancing with and courting Tex became so well-known that George was asked to appear on the *Tonight Show with Johnny Carson*. Unfortunately, just before appearing on national television, George received the news that Tex had been killed by a marauding raccoon. He related this story to a shocked audience, but George's homespun charm won them over and alerted a nation to the plight of the endangered Whooping Crane and ICF efforts on the species' behalf.

Gee Whiz has lived on public display at ICF over the years, although he is currently living in an off-exhibit area. George lightheartedly repeats a story told to him years later by a tour guide at ICF:

> After giving a tour of ICF to a group of school children and relating the entire George and Tex saga, a young boy looked at Gee Whiz with a quizzical expression and asked, "If George is his dad – why don't they look more alike? That bird doesn't look a thing like George."

AFTERWORD

By Dr. George Archibald
Co-founder, International Crane Foundation

Through the pages of this delightful book, we have traveled hundreds and perhaps thousands of years. Let's fast forward a thousand years and imagine the new lore. By then, if the Whooping Cranes have recovered, there will be stories about how hundreds of years ago people dressed in crane costumes to raise the pioneering ancestors. How many cranes will remain in Africa and many parts of Asia where the cranes are now in such peril? Will there be tales about forgotten birds that followed the path of the Passenger Pigeon? Or, will there be stories of restoration?

When we hear the calls of cranes floating down from the heavens, or when we see a parent crane lavishing care on its tiny chick, the magic of the cranes remains to challenge the imagination. I am looking forward to discovering many new stories about cranes, and I hope these magnificent birds will always be here to play their role in the complex web of nature.

ACKNOWLEDGEMENTS

A big thank you to Jennifer Sauer, Jim Harris, George Archibald, Darcy Love, and Mr. & Mrs. Robert Hallam for help making this book possible.

REFERENCE LIST

Afanas'ev, A. N, et al. *Russian Fairy Tales.* 1945. Pantheon Fairy Tale and Folklore Library. New York: Pantheon, 1975.

Ahenakew, Freda, and Sherry Farrell Racette. *Wisahkecahk Flies to the Moon.* Winnepeg: Pemmican, 1999.

Allen, Glover Morrill. *Birds and Their Attributes.* N. Y., New York: Dover Publications, Inc., 1962.

Armstrong, Edward A. "Crane Dance in East and West." *Antiquity* 17 (1943): 71-76.

Armstrong, Edward A. "The Crane in the British Isles and Crane Traditions as Evidence of Cultural Diffusion." *Proceedings, 1978 Crane Workshop:* ed. James C. Lewis. [Fort Morgan, Colo.]: Colorado State University and National Audubon Society, 1979. 237-48.

Armstrong, Edward A. *The Folklore of Birds; an Enquiry into the Origin & Distribution of Some Magico-Religious Traditions.* 2d rev. and enlarged ed. New York: Dover Publications, 1970.

Armstrong, Edward A. *The Life and Lore of the Bird in Nature, Art, Myth, and Literature.* 1st ed. New York: Crown Publishers, 1975.

Austin, Peter, and Norman B. Tindale. "Emu and Brolga, a Kamilaroi Myth." *Aboriginal History Journal* 9.1 (1985): 8-21.

Babbitt, Ellen C., and Ellsworth Young, retold by. *Jataka Tales: Animal Stories.* New York: Appleton Century Crofts, 1940.

Bang, Molly. *The Paper Crane.* New York: William Morrow & Co., 1985.

Bartoli, Jennifer, and Kozo Shimizu. *The Story of the Grateful Crane: a Japanese Folktale.* Chicago: A. Whitman, 1977.

Belting, Natalia M. *The Long-Tailed Bear and Other Indian Legends.* Indianapolis: Bobbs-Merrill, 1961.

Biddle, Steve, and Megumi Biddle. *The Crane's Gift: a Japanese Folktale.* Boston: Barefoot Books, 1994.

Blaauw, Frans Ernst. *A Monograph of the Cranes.* Leiden, London: E. J. Brill. R. H. Porter, 1897.

Blyth, Edward, and Tegetmeier W. B. *The Natural History of the Cranes.* Greatly enlarged, and reprinted, with numerous illustrations ed. [London]: Published for the author by H. Cox and R.H. Porter, 1881.

Bodkin, Odds, and Gennadii Spirin. *The Crane Wife.* 1st ed. San Diego: Harcourt Brace, 1998.

Britton, D. Guyver, and Tsuneo Hayashida. *Japanese Crane: Bird of Happiness.* 1st ed. Tokyo: Kodansha International, 1981.

Bruchac, Joseph. *The Great Ball Game: a Muskogee Story.* New York: Dial Books for Young Readers, 1994.

Catesby, Mark, and Alan Feduccia. *Catesby's Birds of Colonial America.* The Fred W. Morrison Series in Southern Studies. Chapel Hill: University of North Carolina Press, 1985.

Charles, Veronika Martenova. *The Crane Girl.* 1992. Toronto: Stoddart Publishing Co., 1995.

Chen, Kerstin, Jian Jiang Chen, and J. Alison James. *Lord of the Cranes: a Chinese Tale.* New York: North-South Books, 2000.

Chisholm, A. H. *Bird Wonders of Australia.* Sydney, Australia: Angus & Robertson, 1948.

Coerr, Eleanor, and Ed Young. *Sadako.* New York: Putnam, 1993.

Cook, Jean, and Elsie Jimmie. *How the Crane Got Its Blue Eyes: a Yup'Ik Legend.* Bethel, AK: Lower Kuskokwim School District, 1998.

Eastman, Charles Alexander, and Elaine Goodale Eastman. *Wigwam Evenings: Sioux Folk Tales Retold.* Lincoln: University of Nebraska Press, 1990.

Frey, Rodney, and Coeur d'Alene Tribe. *Landscape Traveled by Coyote and Crane: the World of the Schitsu'Umsh (Coeur d'Alene Indians).* Seattle: University of Washington Press, 2001.

Frisbie, Theodore R. "Southwestern Indians and Cranes." *ICF Bugle* 12.1 (1986): 3-5.

Graves, Robert. *The White Goddess: a Historical Grammar of Poetic Myth.* New York: Farrar, Straus and Giroux, 1975.

Grooms, Steve. *Cry of the Sandhill Crane.* Camp and Cottage Birding Collection 3. Minocqua, Wis.: North Word Press, 1991.

Gulik, Robert H. "Lute and Crane." *The Lore of the Chinese Lute: an Essay in the Ideology of the Ch'in.* Tokyo: Sophia University. 141-47.

Hamanaka, Sheila. *Peace Crane.* New York: Morrow Junior Books, 1995.

Hardin, Terri. *Legends and Lore of the American Indians.* New York: Barnes & Noble, 1993.

Harman, Humphrey, and George Ford. *Tales Told Near a Crocodile: Stories From Nyanza.* New York: Viking Press, 1967.

Heady, Eleanor B, and Arvis L Stewart. *Sage Smoke Tales of the Shoshoni-Bannock Indians.* Morristown, NJ: Silver Burdett Press, 1993.

Houlihan, P. F. *The Birds of Ancient Egypt.* Warminster, England: Aris & Phillips, 1986.

Ingersoll, Ernest. *Birds in Legend, Fable, and Folklore.* Detroit: Singing Tree Press, 1968.

Ingpen, Robert R, and Barbara Hayes. *Folk Tales & Fables of Asia & Australia.* New York: Chelsea House Publishers, 1994.

Jacobs, Joseph, and John Dickson Batten. *Indian Folk and Fairy Tales.* Folk and Fairy Tales from Many Lands. New York: Putnam, [1919].

Johnsgard, Paul A. *Cranes of the World.* Bloomington: Indiana University Press, 1983.

Juzhong Zhang, et al. "Oldest Playable Musical Instruments Found at Jiahu Early Neolithic Site in China." *Nature* 401 (1999): 366-68.

Krajewski, Carey. "Phylogenetic Relationships Among Cranes (Aves: Gruidae) Based on DNA Hybridization." Ph.D. thesis. UW-Madison, 1988.

Krutch, Joseph Wood, and Paul S. Eriksson. *A Treasury of Birdlore.* New York: Paul S. Eriksson, Inc, 1962.

Leopold, Aldo. *A Sand County Almanac: With Essays on Conservation from Round River.* 1949. New York: Ballantine Books, 1989.

Leslie, Julia. "A Bird Bereaved: the Identity and Significance of Valmiki's Kraunca." *Journal of Indian Philosophy* 26 (1998): 455-87.

Liang Haitang. "The Distribution of Red-Crowned Cranes in China during the Ming and Qing Dynasties (1368-1911)." *Proceedings 1987 International Crane Workshop:* ed. James T. Harris. Baraboo, Wis: International Crane Foundation, 1991. 184.

Matsutani, Miyoko. *The Crane Maiden* [Tsuru No Ongaeshi]. New York: Parents' Magazine Press, 1968.

Matthiessen, Peter, and Robert Bateman. *The Birds of Heaven: Travels with Cranes.* New York: North Point Press, 2001.

McAtee, W. L. "Birds Pickaback." *The Scientific Monthly* 58.3 (1944): 221-26.

McClintock, Barbara. *Animal Fables from Aesop.* Boston: D.R. Godine, 1991.

McFarlan, Donald, ed. *The Guinness Book of Records, 1989.* 35th ed: Guinness Publishing Ltd.

McLaughlin, Marie L. *Myths and Legends of the Sioux.* Lincoln: University of Nebraska Press, 1990.

McNulty, Faith. *Peeping in the Shell: a Whooping Crane is Hatched.* New York: Harper & Row, 1986.

Meine, Curt, and Richard L Knight. *The Essential Aldo Leopold: Quotations and Commentaries.* Madison, Wis: University of Wisconsin Press, 1999.

Metayer, Maurice. *Tales from the Igloo.* Edmonton: Hurtig Publishers, 1972.

Meyer, David, Silas Head, and Donald McKay. "Indian Bird Identification and Whooping Cranes at Red Earth, Saskatchewan." *The Blue Jay* 32.3 (1974).

"Migration of the Wagtail." *Nature* 23 (1881): 387-88.

Mooney, James. *James Mooney's History, Myths, and Sacred Formulas of the Cherokees: Containing the Full Texts of Myths of the Cherokee (1900) and The Sacred Formulas of the Cherokees (1891) As Published by The Bureau of American Ethnology.* Asheville, N.C: Historical Images, 1992.

Mountford, Charles P. "Brolga, the Dancing Girl." *The Dawn of Time.* Sydney, Australia: Rigby Limited, 1972. 72.

Mountford, Charles P., and Ainslie Roberts, text and illustrations. *The Dreamtime: Australian Aboriginal Myths.* Sydney: Rigby Limited, 1972.

Pande, Suruchi. "Krauncha and Sarasa in Sanskrit Literature." Journal of Ecological Society 16 (2003): 49-51.

Parker, K. Langloh. *Australian Legendary Tales.* London: Bodley Head, 1978.

Rowland, Beryl. *Birds with Human Souls: a Guide to Bird Symbolism.* Knoxville: University of Tennessee Press, 1978. 31-34.

Russell, Nerissa, and Kevin McGowan. "Dance of the Cranes: Crane Symbolism at Çatalhöyük and Beyond." *Antiquity* 77.297 (2003): 445-55.

Sakade, Florence, and Yoshio Hayashi. *Japanese Children's Favorite Stories: Book Two.* Boston, MA: Tuttle Pub, 2004.

Schafer, Edward H. "The Cranes of Mao Shan." *Tantric and Taoist Studies.* ed. Michel Strickmann. Brussels: Institut Belge des Hautes Études Chinoises, 1983. 372-93.

Scobie, Alex. "The Battle of the Pygmies and the Cranes in Chinese, Arab, and North American Indian Sources." *Folklore* 86 (1975): 122-32.

Searcy, Margaret Zehmer, and Lu Celia Wise. *The Race of Flitty Hummingbird and Flappy Crane an Indian Legend*. Tuscaloosa, Ala: Portals Press, 1980.

Seki, Keigo. *Folktales of Japan*. Folktales of the World. Chicago: University of Chicago Press, 1963.

Smith, Anne M, and Alden C Hayes. *Shoshone Tales*. University of Utah Publications in the American West; v. 31. Salt Lake City: University of Utah Press, 1993.

Spring, Madeline K. "The Celebrated Cranes of Po Chu-i." *Journal of the American Oriental Society* 111.1 (1991): 8-18.

Swanton, John Reed. *Myths and Tales of the Southeastern Indians*. Norman: University of Oklahoma Press, 1995.

Topsell, Edward, and Ulisse Aldrovandi. *The Fowles of Heaven or History of Birdes*. Austin: University of Texas, 1972.

Towendolly, Grant, and Marcelle Masson. *A Bag of Bones: Legends of the Wintu Indians of Northern California*. Oakland, Calif: Naturegraph Co, 1966.

Townsend, G. T. *Aesop's Fables*. New York, N.Y: Nelson Doubleday, Inc.

Tyler, Hamilton A. "Sandhill Cranes." *Pueblo Birds and Myths*. Hamilton A. Tyler. Oklahoma: University of Oklahoma Press. 145-51.

Wetmore, Alexander. "Additional Specimens of Fossil Birds from the Upper Tertiary Deposits of Nebraska." *American Museum Novitates*. 302 (1928): 1-5.

Williams, C. A. S. *Chinese Symbolism and Art Motifs: an Alphabetical Compendium of Antique Legends and Beliefs, As Reflected in the Manners and Customs of the Chinese*. 3rd rev. ed: Castle Books, 1974.

Yagawa, Sumiko, and Suekichi Akaba. The Crane Wife. New York: William Morrow, 1981.

INDEX